Metaphysical and Mid-Late Tang Poetry
A Baroque Comparison

Pengfei Wang

Series in Literary Studies

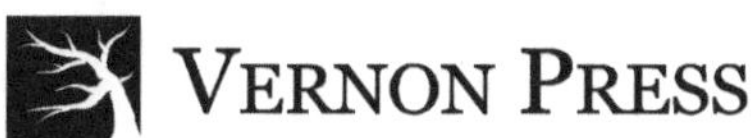

www.vernonpress.com

In the Americas:
Vernon Press
1000 N West Street,
Suite 1200, Wilmington,
Delaware 19801
United States

In the rest of the world:
Vernon Press
C/Sancti Espiritu 17,
Malaga, 29006
Spain

Series in Literary Studies

Library of Congress Control Number: 2019946406

ISBN: 978-1-62273-958-5

Also available: 978-1-62273-773-4 [Hardback]; 978-1-62273-922-6 [PDF, E-Book]

Cover design by Vernon Press using elements designed by starline / Freepik.

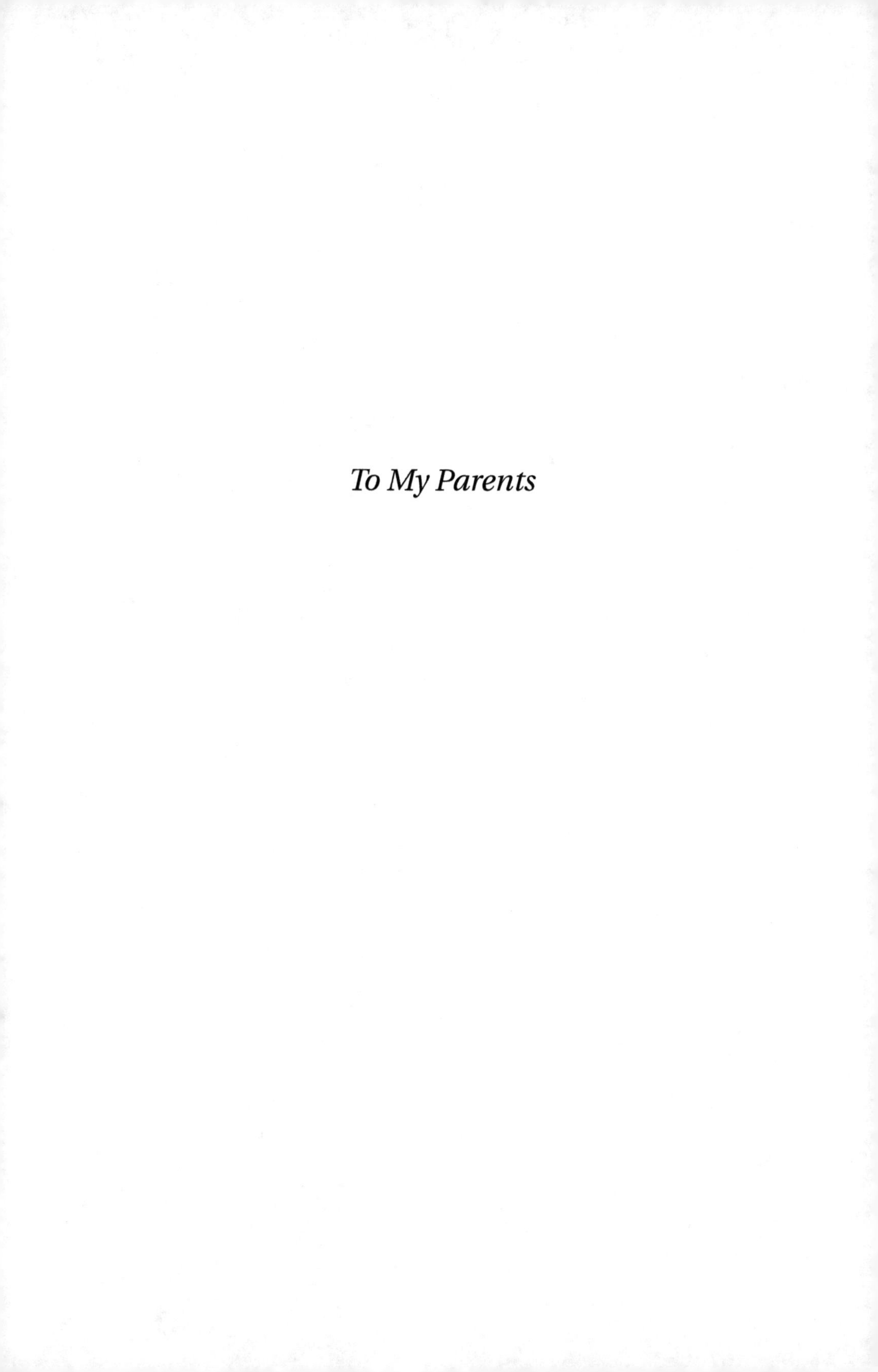

To My Parents

Table of Contents

Preface

Years ago, when I began my PhD study comparing English and Chinese Baroque at the University of Alberta, I wasn't really sure how to go about it. I would have probably gone the way of Tak-wai Wong and James J.Y. Liu – a completely different, even contradictory way. That I did not follow the cliché, I owe it to Professor Massimo Verdicchio. As my PhD supervisor, he not only steered me on the right path and directed the dissertation from which this book comes from, but also made available to me his own work on Li Shangyin and the Baroque, and Benedetto Croce's aesthetics. I have also drawn inspiration from his mentor, Paul de Man, whose definition of modernity seems intuitive to me. All these readings have served me well in understanding Chinese poetry as Baroque rather than literally. I would like to take this opportunity to express my sincere gratitude to Professor Verdicchio. My thanks also goes to Professors Sathya Rao, Waclaw Osadnik, Raleigh Whitinger, Irene Sywenky, and Carrie Smith-Prei for their advice and support.

In my work, I choose to focus on only three metaphysical poets: John Donne, Andrew Marvell, and Richard Crashaw. Accordingly, I have selected three of what I think are the most representative Tang "Baroque" poets: Meng Jiao, Li He and Li Shangyin. Important poets on both sides, like George Herbert and Henry Vaughn for the Metaphysical poets (not to mention other great European Baroque poets), and Han Yu and Bai Juyi for the Tang poets are not examined in this work. It is my hope to include these poets, and others, in my continuous comparative study of the Baroque East and West in the future.

Foreword
by
Massimo Verdicchio
University of Alberta

I consider it an honor to write the Foreword to Pengfei Wang's *Metaphysical and Mid-Late Tang Poetry: A Baroque Comparison,* as I believe that his comparative study on the Baroque is an important critical event. Like all such events, it is characterized by misunderstanding, confusion and opposition. When we are dealing with the Baroque, and with allegory, which is the main characteristic of the baroque, it comes as no surprise. Benedetto Croce probably spoke for Dr. Johnson and John Dryden, and to a certain extent, for contemporary Chinese critics, when he declared the seventeenth century, the century "without poetry" (senza poesia).[1] Similarly, Dr. Johnson and Dryden refused to acknowledge the intrinsically "baroque" character of the poetry of John Donne and Richard Crashaw because it differed from traditional poetry, and called it "metaphysical."[2] James J. Y. Liu and Tak-wai Wong, despite embracing the Baroque as a style to characterize the poetry of Li Shangyin and Meng Jiao, rejected its allegorical character with the result that their comparative analysis failed to provide an adequate analysis of the Baroque in Mid-Late Tang poetry.[3]

We have to be thankful to Georg W. F. Hegel for associating the aesthetic with the symbol and for making allegory an unwelcome term in literary criticism, as the non-poetic and the non-artistic. However, this is only apparently so, as Paul de Man has argued conclusively, demonstrating that for Hegel, the symbol is only the name for the aesthetic phenomenon, which cannot exist independently of allegory. Croce, following Hegel, also rejected allegory and defined it as a form of writing, or a cryptography.[4] However, symbol and allegory are intrinsically related: where there is symbol there is allegory since the symbolic is only the phenomenal manifestation of allegory. For this reason, allegory can be understood as the demystification of the symbol which, at the level of poetic genre, as Nietzsche saw, defines the Baroque style as the decline of traditional symbolic forms in rhetoric, or allegory.[5] Croce, nonetheless, attempted to curb the deleterious spread of allegory, and the Baroque, by confining it to the seventeenth century and denying any further occurrence of baroque in other literary periods. His works on aesthetics, and principally *La Poesia,* are attempts to separate symbol from allegory, and to expunge allegorical forms from poetic ones, without success.

Pengfei Wang's comparative study of English Metaphysical poetry and Mid-Late Tang poetry is an attempt to make up for these earlier shortcomings, both East and West, and restore the Baroque as a legitimate style, and allegory as its essential prosaic and non-artistic form. Only then is it possible to fully appreciate the baroque character of so-called English Metaphysical poetry, as well the apparently difficult and ambivalent poetry of Mid-Late Tang poetry. In this brief introduction I will try to place the analysis of Pengfei Wang in perspective so that the importance and the implications of his ground-breaking work can be properly appreciated.

According to Tak-wai Wong, J. D. Frodsham was the first one to apply the term Baroque to Chinese Literature in a lecture in 1968 on "New Perspectives in Chinese Literature"[6] (Wong 25). Frodsham applied the term to the poetry of Han Yü and Meng Jiao, but his contention was not limited to these poets, or to the post-Renaissance period of the seventeenth century, but to any "recurring historical phenomenon" (quoted in Wong 25). Frodsham, following Nietzsche, defined the Baroque as a decline of art into rhetoric and suggested that tropes such as catachresis, hyperbole and oxymoron in the poetry of Meng Jiao and Lu T'ung might simply be "the decorative overelaboration of a highly conscious, skeptical craftsman, the piling-up of calculated surprises and effects" (quoted in Wong 26). Frodsham argued that these poets share with their Western counterparts a deep concern for the mobility of things, for "Time as a creator and destroyer" (quoted in Wong 26).

Wong, however, felt that Frodsham's definition of the Baroque was too limiting and pejorative, and that his notion of Baroque had to be modified "with a more perceptive reading of the text and a more comprehensive understanding of the term before it could be applied to the study of Chinese literature" (Wong 26). He also extended his critique to James J. Y. Liu's *The Art of Chinese Poetry* who contended that the poetry of Meng Jiao, Lu T'ung and Chia Tao was comparable to English metaphysical poetry in its use of "far-fetched and elaborately developed comparisons," and in its tendency towards "complexity and ambiguity in imagery and syntax" (Wong 28). Wong also took to task Liu's study on the baroque, *The poetry of Li Shang-yin. Ninth-century Baroque Chinese Poet.*[7] Wong claimed that, with the exception of a few paragraphs at the end of Liu's study, the issue of the Baroque was "not properly posed and adequately explored" (Wong 29). He found Liu's view of the Baroque just as restrictive as Frodsham's when he refers to Mid-Late Tang poetry as the period comparable to the seventeenth century in Europe, which was "typified by tendencies toward the exuberant or the grotesque" (Wong 29). Although James Liu was the first to apply the term Baroque to the poetry of Li Shangyin and to the Late Tang period, he did not illustrate, according to Wong, the elements of Li's poetry with specific examples which would identify him as a Baroque poet, at the same level as European Baroque poets.

Wong is also critical of Liu's argument that if Li Shangyin had been a Western poet of the seventeenth century, he would have certainly qualified as a Baroque poet (See Liu 253). Even though the comparison is appropriate, for Wong it was not sufficient to demonstrate the baroque character of Li Shanyin's poetry. In conclusion, Wong resolved that "the term Baroque in Chinese literary studies to date needs more critical perspective and analysis" (Wong 62).[8]

If Tak-wai Wong may be correct in his criticism of James Liu, his own version of the Baroque did not bring us any closer to understanding these poets. While Wong differs from Liu in what constitutes baroque poetry, their approach is similar and very traditional. This is clear in how they approach translation. For James Liu an adequate re-creation of the original entails the literalization of the original, insofar as this is possible. His aim as a translator is to favor those who cannot read Chinese in the original: "to translate a poem is to try to reproduce the verbal structure of the original, so that the reader of the translation will respond to it, as far as possible, in the same way that the translator responded to the original poem, thereby re-creating, to some extent, what the poet originally created" (Liu 34).

Liu believes that we can make sense of poems "without committing ourselves to a definite theory," but when one translates the choice cannot be naïve since it is dictated, inevitably, by the preconceptions of the translator. (Liu 32) This is true of the Chinese language, where pronouns and other grammatical elements are placed at the discretion of the translator. In addressing these difficulties, Liu describes the "eternal dilemma" of the translator to decide between a "literal" and "literary" translation. By the term "literary" Liu means figural or allegorical. Every translator in deciding whether to translate literally or figuratively "steers a dangerous course between the Scylla of dull pedantry and the Charybdis of irresponsible dilettantism" (Liu 35). In any case, one should steer clear of the "literary" because its "excessive freedom" makes translation not only "undesirable, but at times impossible" (Liu 35).

Liu argues that a poem "can mean more than one thing at the same time, on different levels" (Liu 32), which implies that a symbolic reading is to be preferred to an allegorical one. The symbolic allows for the possibility of different interpretations, while the allegorical involves "definite identification of elements in a poem with actual persons and events" (Liu 32). Liu's definition of allegory is somewhat different from Hegel's and Croce's, but it amounts to the same. In his example, allegory is like personification, an enigma to be resolved. Instead of considering a poem as "an autobiographical revelation," he writes, it is better to take each one "dramatically" (Liu 32). This approach requires the reconstruction of a dramatic situation that makes sense of a poem in more than one way, without identifying the main characters of the drama. He gives the example of Shakespeare's Dark Lady, whose identity is not necessary to understand the dramatic situation of the sonnets. The actual agents are not important, what is relevant is the extent to which the poet allows us to enter “into the worlds of moral indignation, conjugal affection, and paternal love that can afford us some guide to the value of these poems as poetry” (Liu 32). In the case of Shakespeare's “Dark Lady” knowing her identity would not add to our understanding and evaluation of the sonnets: “All we need is the dramatic situation implicit in the sonnets themselves” (Liu 32). For this reason, Liu dismisses the literary, or allegory, as irrelevant and opts in favor of a literal or symbolic approach. Yet, if Shakespeare's Dark Lady, instead of a she, turns out to be a “he,” as it has often been suggested, would that not make all the difference to a reading of the sonnets?

Indeed, the navigation between the literal and the literary, or the figural, is like navigating between Scylla and Charybdis: almost an impossibility, both for the translator and the interpreter. However, doing away with the literary would be like getting rid of Scylla or Charybdis, and this is an even greater impossibility. The “figural,” or allegorical, is undesirable and impossible precisely because it is difficult, if not impossible, to read, unlike the symbolical which relies on the literal that makes reading more accessible and enjoyable. Liu's symbolic approach promotes a literal meaning, at many levels, to resolve the ambiguity which characterizes, in this case, the poetry of Li Shangyin. However, this approach does not bring us closer to understanding Li's poetry or baroque poetry. What makes the comparison possible between Li and poets as diverse as Quevedo, Marino, Crashaw, Gryphius or Góngora, are not the “baroque” elements which they may have in common, as Wong suggests, (Wong 26) but the allegorical nature of their poetry, or, which is the same, the manner in which the apparent symbolic representation of their poetry is interrupted or interfered with.

Pengfei Wang's study takes its starting point from this problematic by analyzing Mid-Late Tang poetry as Baroque or allegorical poetry, comparing it to English Metaphysical poetry. The comparison is not based on the baroque elements, which their poetry may have in common, but on an analysis of their poems as allegorical compositions, and by means of a discussion of conceits and rhetorical devices. The first chapter analyzes three poems of John Donne, Andrew Marvell and Richard Crashaw, emphasizing their baroque characteristics. The second chapter does the same with analyses of three poems of Meng Jiao, Li He and Li Shangyin. Their similarities and differences are the subject of the third chapter, which is a theoretical chapter on Baroque conceits. While the second chapter is an original reading of the three Mid-Late

Tang poets, the first chapter is an important contribution to the study of Donne, Marvell, and Crashaw, as Baroque poets.

Mid-Late Tang poetry, which has always been read literally, or symbolically, gains a new perspective when read rhetorically or allegorically. Pengfei Wang provides for each poem two translations: one literal, the other literary, or figural. The difference is clear in the analysis of a true Baroque poet like Meng Jiao, but also in Li Shangyin and Li He. The trope of allusion, which characterizes much of Li Shangyin's poetry, is a baroque device meant to displace the apparent symbolic character of poetic representation; in Li He, instead, the Baroque element is evident in the ironic displacement of ancient poetic forms.

The two poetic schools are discussed in Chapter III. This is the theoretical chapter where Pengfei Wang deals with the theories of metaphor of Emanuele Tesauro and Matteo Peregrini, which were well-known in seventeenth-century Europe, and had an influence on Baroque poetry in Italy and Spain. English literary criticism, however, was, and still is, reluctant to adopt these theories or to accept poets like Donne, Marvell and Crashaw as Baroque poets. "Baroque" is still not an acceptable term since, as I have indicated, it is not just a question of labels but of poetics and, reading allegorically. Chapter III also deals with Baroque conceits and contrasts their use in both Metaphysical and Mid-Late Tang poetry.

The importance of Pengfei Wang's study for Chinese literature, and for literary criticism in general, lies not only in the study of these poets and poems, a choice which is necessarily limited by time and space (one hopes that in the future the choice will be extended to other poets and poems), but in his contribution to Comparative Literary Studies East and West, which began with Frodsham, James Liu and Tak-way Wong. There is understandable resistance to the Baroque, as there was to Frodsham's early vision of a Chinese literary history on the model of Western literary history. This need not be the case. It is true that a different periodization of Chinese Literary History could make it more comprehensible to a Westerner and it wouldn't radically alter the way its poetry, or literature, is read. However, if we accept Nietzsche's definition of Baroque as a poetic style, which can be found in any period and in any country, it will be easier to approach Chinese poetry, once we keep in mind that, whether Western or Chinese, behind its symbolic façade, it will still be a rhetorical or Baroque composition. All poetry, that is, all great poetry, is always allegorical, and will always be Baroque poetry. Despite our deepest wish, poetry can never be symbolic because, the symbol is only "a veil" that persists for as long as we choose to remain blind to the essential prosaic, or allegorical, nature of poetry, and art. It is to Pengfei Wang's great merit that this comparative study of English Metaphysical and Mid-Late Tang poetry has shown the way to a deeper and more rewarding reading of these great poets and their poetry, both East and West, which, it is hoped, will inspire others to follow his lead.

Notes

[1] Benedetto Croce. *Storia dell'eta Barocca in Italia. Pensiero, poesia e letteratura e vita morale.* Bari: G. Laterza, 1957.

[2] Samuel Johnson. "Life of Abraham Cowley." *Lives of the English Poets.* London: J. M. Dent, 1925; John Dryden. "A Discourse of the Original and Progress of Satire." *Of Dramatic poesy, and other critical essays.* Ed. George Watson. London: J. M. Dent, 1962, 2: 144.

[3] James J. Y. Liu. *The Poetry of Li Shang-yin. Ninth-century Baroque Chinese Poet.* Chicago and London: The University of Chicago Press, 1969; Tak-wai Wong. "Toward Defining Chinese Baroque Poetry." *Tamkang Review,* vol. viii, April 1977, no.1, 25-72;

[4] Georg W. F. Hegel. *Aesthetics. Lectures on Fine Arts.* Oxford: At the Clarendon press, 1975, 499-501. For Paul de Man, see "Sign and Symbol in Hegel's *Aesthetics.*" *Aesthetic Ideology.* Edited with an Introduction by Andrzej Warminski. Minneapolis/London: The University of Minnesota Press, 1996, 91-104. For Benedetto Croce see, *La Poesia. Introduzione alla critica e storia della poesia e della letteratura,* a.c.d. Giuseppe Galasso. Milan: Adelphi, 1994. The English translation is by Giovanni Gullace. *Poetry and Literature. An Introduction to its Criticism and History.* Carbondale and Edwardsville: Southern Illinois University Press, 1981. For the reference to allegory, see Croce, 227, Gullace, 40.

[5] Nietzsche, "On the Baroque style." *Human, All too Human. A Book for free spirits.* Translated by R. J. Hollingdale. Introduction by Richard Schacht. Cambridge: Cambridge University Press, 1986, 1996, 245-46.

[6] J. D. Frodsham, *New Perspectives in Chinese Literature.* Canberra: Australian National U. Press, 1970. For Tak-wai Wong see note 3.

[7]James J. Y. Liu. *The Art of Chinese Poetry.* London: Routledge & Kegan Paul, 1962; *The Poetry of Li Shang-yin. Ninth-century Baroque Chinese Poet.* Chicago and London: The University of Chicago Press, 1969.

[8] Wong also discusses the use of the baroque by Kalvodová and Mc Leod (36-45) and the Baroque in the poetry of Meng Jiao and Han Yü. (46-60).

Introduction

Toward Redefining Chinese Baroque Poetry through Comparison

> Don't reproach us our lack of clarity
> because this is what we do. (Pascal)

A comparison between English Metaphysical and Mid-Late Tang poetry is only possible if we understand by Baroque a poetic style that occurs in opposition to traditional, mimetic or symbolic forms of art. This definition, which comes from Nietzsche, describes the Baroque, which is usually associated with the plastic arts and the poetry of the seventeenth century, as a style that can occur in any period and in any place, whether in England, or Europe, or in China. Nietzsche writes that the Baroque style emerges when "any great art starts to fade, whenever the demands in the art of classic expression grow too great."[1] He gives the example of Michelangelo, whom he calls the father or grandfather of Italian Baroque, and the artist who broke from the artistic mold of classical rules of art. The Baroque style may lack the nobility we confer on the symbol and on symbolic representations, nonetheless, it is always to allegory that we turn to understand the artistic and the poetic; just as we turn to Baroque poets to learn about our modernity, as I hope to show in my discussion of the English Metaphysical and Mid-Late Tang poets. The Baroque does not belong solely to the seventeenth century in Europe, or ends with it. It is not an artistic style which is determined by history or literary history. On the contrary, an historical approach, which is always symbolic, entails the repression of allegory, and the end of the Baroque.

The Baroque, when understood as allegory, has not fared too well with literary critics or philosophers. Benedetto Croce, the twentieth-century Italian critic and philosopher, regarded the Italian seventeenth century as a "century without poetry" (un secolo senza poesia)".[2] He denied that the Baroque can be found in the work of writers other than the seventeenth century. For Croce, Baroque poetry is allegorical poetry and as such, it was neither poetic nor artistic, because art is symbolic. Allegory, on the contrary, is non-artistic, anti-artistic, and should be avoided at all costs. Croce spent a lifetime separating symbol from allegory in poetry, but always without success.[3] Croce derived his concept of allegory from Hegel who, in the *Aesthetics* identified the artistic with the symbol, and allegory with the non-artistic.[4] He defined allegory as "*frostig und kahl,*" (*icy and bleak)* and dismissed it as "a product of the intellect and not of concrete intuition and of the deep feeling of imagination, and lacking inherent seriousness, prosaic, and distant from art" (Hegel 501). Following Hegel, Croce wrote that "Allegory is not a direct form of spiritual expression, only a kind of writing or cryptography" (Croce's *La Poesia* 227*)*.[5]

In Art criticism, the Baroque is usually confused with Mannerism, an exaggeration of form found in the Late Renaissance, however, they are the expression of two dominant and opposing artistic styles. The former emphasizes unity, the latter vitality and multiplicity. There have been many definitions of Baroque. Jorge Luis Borges defined it as "that style that deliberately exhausts (or at least tries to) its own possibilities, and that borders on self-caricature."[6] Benedetto Croce, in his study on the Baroque mentioned above, thought that the term derived from "Barocco," after the fourth mode of the second figure in the nomenclature of syllogisms in Scholasticism. (If A=B and some C does not equal B, then some C does not equal A). He also thought that the term came from the Portuguese for *perrola barroca*: a jeweller's term for an irregular shaped or flawed pearl.[7] Rene Wellek, despairing of a definition, after presenting all possible variations, concluded that "the Baroque has provided an aesthetic term which has helped us to understand the literature of the time, and which will help us to break the dependence of most literary history from periodization derived from political and social history" (Wellek 97).[8]

In England, poets like John Donne, who seemed to stray from accepted and traditional poetic forms, were declared non-poetic and prosaic.[9] When John Dryden read Crashaw and Dr. Johnson read John Donne, they found the poetry of these poets distasteful and abstract. They called it "metaphysical" but they might as well have called it "Baroque," as with the rest of Europe. In his *Lives of the English Poets*, Dr. Johnson suggested that metaphysical wit was the result of a "discordia concors: a combination of dissimilar images, or discovery of occult resemblances in things apparently unlike."[10] John Dryden in "A Discourse of the Original and Progress of Satire" (1693) disapproved of John Donne's wit and satire: "Would not Donne's satires, which abound with so much wit, appear more charming if he had taken care of his words, and of his numbers? But he followed Horace so very close that of necessity he must fall with him. And I may safely say it of this present age, that if we were not so great wits as Donne, yet certainly we are better poets."[11] They had to wait for T. S. Eliot to counter Dr. Johnson's negative assessment and to recognize their rightful place in the history of English poetry, and reinstate them as modern poets.[12] However, contemporary criticism is still divided as to whether to keep the name "metaphysical" or to call them "Baroque" poets, as the rest of the European poets of the seventeenth century.[13]

English scholars have listed the main characteristics of English Metaphysical poetry: conceit and emblem, theatricality, antithesis and paradox, quiddity (a form of syllogism), contrast between erotic love and religious love and, in particular, an opposition to the Renaissance poetic ideal of "*ars est celare artem.*" The latter was also the major aspect that Samuel Johnson found objectionable in Baroque poetry that, in his view, perverted the doctrine of "*ars est celare artem*" into its very opposite. However, this was, precisely, the distinctive character of Metaphysical or Baroque poets for whom true art is *ars est praesentare artem*, in a radical break from traditional Renaissance poetry, and the influence of Petrarch and Petrarchism. However, at stake, in hiding or concealing art, is not simply a question of approach but an aesthetic one, of symbol or allegory.

The question of Baroque can be understood as a version of the quarrel between the ancients and the moderns, the classical and the modern but the differences are not so clear cut. If the Baroque can be said to be decidedly on the side of the ancients, as a seventeenth-century aesthetic which is superseded by more modern poetic forms, such as Romanticism and Modernism, as an artistic style and not as a historical period, the Baroque is on the side of the moderns. The in-between character of the Baroque, which situates it both in the past and in the present, is what accounts for the complexity of the Baroque but also for its modernity. As Paul de Man has defined it, "Modernity exists in the form of a desire to wipe out whatever came earlier, in the hope of reaching, at last, a point that could be called a true present, a point of origin that marks a new departure. This combined interplay of deliberate forgetting with an action that is also an origin reaches the full power of the idea of Modernity."[14] In severing itself from the past, the Baroque also severs itself from the present. Modernity, explains de Man, confronts us at all times with an unsolvable paradox: "Literature exists at the same time in the modes of error and truth, it both betrays and obeys its own mode of being" (de Man, *Blindness and Insight*, 163-64). Literature, understood as allegory, or as Baroque, partakes of both past and present, as ancient and modern, and, of course, as both symbol and allegory.

The modernity of Baroque, or Baroque literature, or Baroque lyric, is characterized by its non-mimetic, non-symbolic form or, simply, by allegory. As such, Baroque's modernity is determined by its distance from a symbolic form, from the way it departs and undermines a concept of art as symbol. As allegory, the Baroque undermines and obscures the specific literal meaning of a representation open to (symbolic) understanding. On the other hand, allegory contains a representational, or symbolic, element that allows for understanding but only in order to show that the understanding it reaches is necessarily in error. Since allegory can only blindly repeat the earlier model without finally understanding it, it is, essentially, the negation of modernity. However, our lack of understanding is, paradoxically, what makes it modern. The less we understand a poet, writes de Man, the more he is misinterpreted and made to say the opposite of what he said, the more he is truly modern, that is, different from what we, mistakenly, think we are ourselves (de Man, *Blindness and Insight*, 164). This paradox defines the modernity of the Baroque and its essence as allegory, as well as, its constitutive symbolic character.

One other critic who has made an important contribution to the study and the understanding of Baroque is Walter Benjamin. Although his study, *The Origin of German Tragic Drama*, was meant to describe the German Baroque Mourning Drama, the German *Trauerspiel*, his work makes an important contribution to the relation of Baroque and allegory, and to notions of social decline and decay.[15] Central to his view is the notion of a divine concept of violence that interrupts the course of time and initiates a future in a long tragic "suspense." In this suspense is inscribed what has been called "the politics of suspense," or "the suspension of the political," founded on the belief of an absolute break, or rupture, with the past. In Benjamin, this radical abolition, inversion and reversal of the past, is explicitly established in the German classical Baroque.[16] However, only the poetry of Meng Jiao seems to come close to Benjamin's concept of allegory, as I point out in my discussion of the poet in chapter two.

Chinese poets of the Mid-Late Tang experienced a similar case of ostracism from their contemporaries. Although their poetry was admired, the poetry of Meng Jiao, Li He and Li Shangyin, which I discuss in this study, went unappreciated and almost forgotten until they were discovered by later poets and recognized not only as great poetry, but also as modern poetry, or "Baroque" poetry. According to Tak-wai Wong, J. D. Frodsham was the first to apply the term Baroque to Chinese Literature, and to Tang poets, in particular, in a lecture in 1968 on *New Perspectives in Chinese Literature*.[17] Frodsham applied the term "Baroque" to the poetry of Han Yu and Meng Jiao but his definition was not limited to the Tang poets or to the post-Renaissance period of the seventeenth century, but was applicable to any "recurring historical phenomenon." Frodsham followed Nietzsche and his view of Baroque style, as I have indicated, namely, that Baroque implies a decline in art into rhetoric and that "tropes and catachresis, hyperboles and oxymorons" in the poetry of Meng Jiao and Lu Tong might simply be "the decorative overelaboration of a highly conscious, skeptical craftsman, the pilings-up of calculated surprises and effects." Frodsham argued that what these Chinese poets share with their Western counterparts is a deep concern with the mobility of things, with "Time as a creator and destroyer" (Wong 26).

For Wong, however, Frodsham's definition of Baroque is too limited and negative. He believes that his concept of the Baroque has to be modified "with a more perceptive reading of the text, and a more comprehensive understanding of the term before it can be applied to the study of Chinese literature" (Wong 26). Wong's critique also extends to James J. Y. Liu's *The Art of Chinese Poetry* (1962)[18] where Liu contends that the poetry of Meng Jiao, Lu Tong and Jia Tao is comparable to English metaphysical poetry in its use of "farfetched and elaborately developed comparisons, and in its tendency towards complexity and ambiguity in imagery and syntax" (in Wong 28). Wong is also critical of Liu's *The poetry of Li Shang-yin. Ninth-century Baroque Chinese Poet*, the first comprehensive study not only of Chinese Baroque poetry but also of a major Late Tang poet.[19] With the exception of a few paragraphs at the end of Liu's study, for Wong, the issue of Baroque is "not properly posed and adequately explored" (Wong 29). He finds a similar restrictive view of Baroque as he noted in Frodsham, when Liu refers to Mid-Late Tang poetry, as the period comparable to the seventeenth century in Europe, "typified by tendencies toward the exuberant or the grotesque" (Wong 29). For Wong, Liu did not illustrate sufficiently, and with specific examples, the elements of Li Shangyin's poetry which would identify him as a Baroque poet on the same level as European Baroque poets. He is also critical of Liu's claim that if Li Shangyin had been a Western poet of the seventeenth century, he would have qualified as a Baroque poet. This historical fact alone, Wong rightly states, would not have made Li a Baroque poet.

Despite his critique of Frodsham and James Liu, Wong himself does not make a better case for a Baroque reading of Li Shangyin, or other Mid-Late Tang poets. Like Liu, Wong seems to believe that a simple correspondence between Chinese and Western poets suffices to establish a Baroque comparison. He believes that it suffices to show that Tang poets share with the English Metaphysical poets similar characteristics to qualify them as Baroque poets. These include time, historical or mythological allusions, exploitation of conventional verse, momentary resolution of opposites, the use of conceit, and the use of language (Wong 33-35). However, these characteristics are not exclusive to the Baroque and can be said to apply to any poem without, necessarily, defining it as Baroque. Wong's comparisons with metaphysical poets are too general to apply to a reading of a Baroque poem. It also does not help to know that Li Shangyin, like Donne, as Wong claims, is "remarkable in his intricate use of diction and dramatic situation;" that like Crashaw he is capable "to interpenetrate the metaphysical and the high baroque style with potentially sensual images"; or that like Góngora he is able to use "innumerable classical allusions in a constant periphrastic style." These associations with established Western Baroque poets may contribute to regard Tang poets as Baroque, but do not help us in reading their poetry as such. The same can be said for Wong's claim that "Li Shangyin's attempts to cover the enormous range between temporality and eternity, emotion and intellect, illusion and intellect, the duplicity of language and style, etc., are all strong indications of the baroque" (Wong 36). These indications are descriptive and not critical and while they may define Li Shangyin's poetry as Baroque poetry, they don't help us to read it as such.

The main difficulty in reading Li Shangyin's poetry, or any Chinese poetry as Baroque lies not in the similar devices that they may have in common with Western Baroque poets, or even English Metaphysical poets, but in the allegorical character of their poetry. While Wong and Liu can claim that Li Shangyin is a Baroque poet, they reject allegory as an artistic mode, and read his poems as if they were traditional and symbolic. As critics and translators, in deciding between a "literal" or symbolical translation and a "literary" or allegorical one, they always choose the literal. Liu believes that one should steer clear of the "literary," or allegorical, because its "excessive freedom" makes translation not only "undesirable, but at times impossible" (Liu, *Poetry of Li Shangyin*, 35). Indeed, the navigation between the literal and the literary, the figural or allegorical, is difficult to chart, both for the translator and the interpreter. However doing away with the figural is not only undesirable, but also impossible. Both Wong and Liu believe that a literal and symbolic approach will enable them to steer clear of the difficulties of reading the poems as Baroque but, in so doing, they only encounter a web of ambiguities and contradictions which they cannot resolve.

Since allegory is what characterizes and defines the Baroque style of poetry, both in the seventeenth century and in ninth century Mid-Late Tang poetry, in opposition to traditional and symbolic forms, reading the poems symbolically is reading them against the grain, or misreading them. The problem with Wong's and Liu's approaches is that they attempt to read a Baroque poem as a traditional poem, or, which is the same, to read an allegorical poem symbolically. Once the figural, or the allegorical, is displaced in Liu, and allegory and rhetoric have been dismissed in Wong, how can they hope to read the poetry of Li Shangyin, or of any other Baroque poet? Both critics overlook the essentially rhetorical or allegorical mode of the Baroque, and they choose to read it symbolically, as a dramatized narrative. What characterizes a Baroque poem, instead, is the way it departs from classical or symbolic forms of art and privileges tropes over the meaning they produce, poetics over hermeneutics, allegory over symbol.

A similar negative attitude towards allegory is found in most translators and commentators of the Tang poets that I discuss in this study. Stephen Owen, the well-known Sinologist, critic and translator, shares a similar aversion to allegory, which he regards as not being an acceptable subject for poetry, but only a superficial and incidental supplement to artistic form.[20] For him, allegory is a pejorative mode of representation that we need not be concerned with. Frodsham, however, as I mentioned, was one of the first to acknowledge these Mid-Late Tang poets as Baroque and allegorical poets. He understood with Nietzsche that Baroque style is not a historical concept but a style of art that is predicated on the demystification of art as a symbol. The poetry of poets like Donne, Marvell, Crashaw, Meng Jiao, Li He and Li Shangyin, which I discuss here, does not depend on a mimetic representation of external reality, as one could claim for the classical or traditional modes of symbolical art. Their models are folklore, myths, or even traditional poems, which they re-adapt and re-construct, but never imitate. This poetry stands alone as an allegory of the impossibility of imitating these models and this is what makes them modern. For this reason, their poems are not really "lyrics" in the traditional sense. They are non-lyrics, or anti-lyrics; they are prosaic or allegorical, or simply Baroque. That is why we read them as poets of the past but also as poets of our modernity.

In addition to this Introduction, my study consists of three chapters, a brief conclusion and a bibliography. The first chapter is on English Metaphysical poets, the second on the Mid-Late Tang poets, the third chapter is a comparative analysis of their conceits. The first chapter investigates three poems by John Donne, Andrew Marvell and Richard Crashaw respectively. In this chapter, my aim is not to provide a critical analysis of their poems, but I have limited myself to give the standard reading of their poems, and to identify the main conceits that characterize them as Baroque. I have also added a brief discussion of how contemporary scholars approach and analyze these Metaphysical poets in the light of modern literary theory and theories of the Baroque.

On the other hand, in chapter two, in the analysis of the three Mid-Late Tang poets, the issue is translation. The three poets I deal with, Meng Jiao, Li He and Li Shangyin, make it necessary that I provide my own translation for each of the three poems I discuss, in order to better confront and relate them to the original. At the same time, I also try to comment on two other translations of each poem as complimentary to my own. However, finding two translations was not always an easy task. For example, in the case of Li Shangyin's "Written on a Monastery Wall," I could only find two translations by Arthur Cooper and by A. C. Graham. Whenever possible, I might have chosen the best two translations other than my own but, as it turned out, one translation was always too literal and faithful to the original and the other more interpretative and figural. For instance, in the case of "Written on a Monastery Wall," Cooper's translation of the poem seems to have been prompted by A. C. Graham's more literal translation. Cooper does not tell us why, of course, but he must have felt that A. C. Graham did not translate the poem adequately. He is a well-known translator and a very good one, but this particular translation does not do justice to the poem. I choose to create my own translations to the poems and leave further discussion of the translations to the analysis of the poem in Chapter Two.

The translations I have encountered and commented most often are by Stephen Owen and J. D. Frodsham who have devoted most of their work to translating the poets I deal with. Stephen Owen has translated almost everything by Li Shangyin and Meng Jiao, while Frodsham has translated Li He and Meng Jiao. For Meng Jiao I have also commented on David Hinton who is a good and reliable translator. For Meng Jiao I have also referenced the study of Tak-wai Wong who, compared to Hinton's more liberal, gives a more literal interpretation. For Li He, I have also cited the research of Fusheng Wu who, compared to Frodsham is also more literal. The difference between Frodsham and Owen does not need elaboration. Stephen Owen is an excellent scholar and translator but his translations tend to be very literal and leave the reader to guess much of the poem. Frodsham, on the other hand, who, as I mentioned earlier, is an early promoter of ninth-century Tang poetry as Baroque, has always the Western reader in mind and his translations tend to provide a more readable, if less accurate translation. He was a well-known Sinologist, scholar and translator, and the first to come up with the idea that there are some periods in Chinese literature that could be defined as Baroque. Actually, this idea was part of a greater plan to restructure Chinese Literary history on the model of Western Literary history. This plan did not receive much enthusiasm from Chinese scholars but his enthusiasm is clear in his translations, which attempt to read Chinese poems as Western poems. Even for me, who am a Chinese speaker, J. D. Frodsham's translations have been of great help. All the translators, each in his own way, have been of great help to me to read the original, and all of them have given me not only a better understanding of the poem, but have also enabled me to explain why, in my view, this poetry should be considered Baroque.

The third chapter has been the most difficult to write. The comparative analysis of the English Metaphysical poets and Mid-Late Tang poets could not be based on comparing, supposedly, their similar devices, as Wong and Liu tried to do. Since my claim is that the poems are "Baroque" because they are allegorical, it remained for me to show how their conceit illustrated their allegorical style. I decided to discuss their conceits, or their wit, the main themes they deal with, and the poetic context in which they wrote. In other words, what rhetorical elements identify these poems as allegory, that is, as narratives of the impossibility of reading them for the literal meaning they seem to refer to; that is, as symbolic poems. I hope I have succeeded in showing, at least, how these poems cannot be read symbolically, as lyrics, but as allegories, or as non-lyrics.

Notes

[1] Friedrich Nietzsche. "On the Baroque style." *Human, All too Human. A Book for free spirits* Translated by R. J. Hollingdale (Cambridge: Cambridge University Press, 1986), 245-46.
[2] See the Introduction to Benedetto Croce. *Storia dell'eta Barocca in Italia* (Bari: G. Laterza, 1957).
[3] For Croce's lifelong debate on allegory see M. Verdicchio. *Naming Things. Aesthetics Philosophy and History in Benedetto Croce* (Naples: La citta del Sole, 2000).
[4] See Croce. *La poesia* (Bari: G. Laterza, 1936), 227. On closer analysis, both Hegel and Croce identify art with allegory and the symbol as the name of the artistic only apparently. See Hegel's Lectures on Fine Arts, 499-501. For further discussion see Paul de Man. "Sign and Symbol in Hegel's Aesthetics." Aesthetic Ideology, (Minneapolis: University of Minnesota Press, 1996), 91-104.
[5] See Croce. *La poesia* (Bari: G. Laterza, 1936), 227.
[6] See Jorge L. Borges. *Universal History of Infamy* (New York: Dutton, 1978).
[7] See Croce's Introduction to *Storia dell'età barocca in Italia* (Bari: G. Laterza, 1957).
[8] For a good survey of writings on the Baroque, see Rene Wellek's "The Concept of Baroque in Literary Scholarship," 77-109. See also his bibliography of works on the Baroque from 1888-1946.
[9] For a lengthy discussion of the English Metaphysical poets see Rolf P. Lessenich, "The "Metaphysicals": English Baroque Literature in Context."
[10] Samuel Johnson. "Life of Abraham Cowley." Lives of the English Poets, quoted in Wellek, "Concept of Baroque", 90.
[11] John Dryden. "A Discourse of the Original and Progress of Satire." Ed. Watson (1962), 2: 144.
[12] For a discussion of T. S. Eliot's contribution see the next chapter.
[13] See my discussion of recent contemporary criticism on the "English Metaphysical poets" in chapter one.
[14] See Paul de Man. "Literary History and Literary Modernity," *Blindness and Insight*, (Minneapolis: University of Minnesota Press, 1983), 148.
[15] Walter Benjamin. *The Origin of German Tragic Drama* (London: Verso. 2009).
[16] For a different view of Benjamin's concept of the Baroque see my discussion of Hugh Grady in chapter one. Grady associates Benjamin's poetics with those of Baudelaire and with those of John Donne.

[17] Tak-wai Wong. "Toward Defining Chinese Baroque Poetry." *Tamkang Review*, 25-72. For J. D. Frodsham, see his New Perspectives in Chinese Literature, quoted in Wong 25.
[18] James J. Y. Liu. *The Art of Chinese Poetry*, (Chicago: The University of Chicago Press, 1962).
[19]James J. Y. Liu. *The Poetry of Li Shang-yin. Ninth-century Baroque Chines Poet*, (Chicago: The University of Chicago Press, 1969).
[20] For a reading of Owen's aesthetics see Verdicchio's "Under Western Literary Eyes."

Chapter 1

English Metaphysical poetry

Metaphysical poetry is usually described as intellectual poetry characterized by bold and elaborate metaphorical conceits and wit, subtle thoughts with learned themes. Herbert Grierson compares their conceits with those of the Elizabethans as being more intellectual and less verbal, more learned and argumentative and, above all, subtle in the evolution of their lyrics. Above all their greatest achievement is "the peculiar blend of passion and thought, feeling and reaction."[1] The term "metaphysical" was coined by Samuel Johnson in the eighteenth century as a derogatory term for a type of poetry that varied radically from the previous Elizabethan model. Since then, it has become a general term for a type of poetry that has often been characterized as Baroque, since its themes and conceits are similar to the Baroque poetry of other European countries.[2] In this chapter, I discuss three poems of the three most representative metaphysical poets, John Donne, Andrew Marvell and Richard Crashaw, by focusing mainly on their themes, use of conceits and wit.

John Donne: The Erotic and the Divine

John Donne is considered the leading figure of the metaphysical poets. His themes deal with the conflict between soul and body, spirituality and sensuality, which we find expressed in the three poems I have chosen: "The Flea," "The Good Morrow" and "The Sun Rising." Donne makes use of a single elaborate metaphorical conceit in order to develop an always deeper understanding of the speaker's emotions. The three poems I have selected are from the *Songs and Sonnets*, which is mostly a collection of love lyrics.[3] The themes of these love lyrics vary, but most of them focus on the conflict between body and soul, spirituality and sensuality in the microcosm of love, through images that are geographical, astronomical and cosmological. The best representative of this theme is, of course, "The Flea" (Shawcross, 127).

The Flea

Before Donne, "the flea" was already a popular and widely used conceit in erotic poems in sixteenth-century Europe. The reason the flea has strong erotic connotations, besides the impact of Ovid, is the popular view that sex is the mingling of bloods and the flea's bloodthirsty nature makes possible for them to drink blood from different people, and mix their blood in their body.[4] This belief makes the flea an excellent erotic metaphor that John Donne exploits to his advantage to seduce his woman.

The Flea

Mark but this flea, and mark in this,
How little that which thou deniest me is;
It sucked me first, and now sucks thee,
And in this flea our two bloods mingled be;
Thou know'st that this cannot be said
A sin, nor shame, nor loss of maidenhead,
Yet this enjoys before it woo,
And pampered swells with one blood made of two,
And this, alas, is more than we would do.
Oh stay, three lives in one flea spare,

Where we almost, nay more than married are.
This flea is you and I, and this
Our marriage bed, and marriage temple is;
Though parents grudge, and you, w'are met,
And cloistered in these living walls of jet.
Though use make you apt to kill me,
Let not to that, self-murder added be,
And sacrilege, three sins in killing three.
Cruel and sudden, hast thou since

Purpled thy nail, in blood of innocence?
Wherein could this flea guilty be,
Except in that drop which it sucked from thee?
Yet thou triumph'st, and say'st that thou
Find'st not thy self, nor me the weaker now;
'Tis true; then learn how false, fears be:
Just so much honor, when thou yield'st to me,
Will waste, as this flea's death took life from thee.

In the poem, Donne creates a dramatic scene the moment that he finds that a flea has just bit them. He compares the minute size of the flea with the denial he gets from his beloved: "how little that which thou deny'st me is." He tells his woman about the flea and its tendency to mingle blood in order to suggest the possibility of their having sex. As she refuses, he tells her that the mingling of their bloods in the body of the flea is not a sin: "cannot be said/ A sin, or shame or loss of maidenhead,/Yet this enjoys before it woo." And because the flea has drunk both their blood it has already united them in a way that they do not dare to do: "more than we would do."

In the second stanza, the poet stops his beloved from killing the flea. In the flea, there are three lives: his, hers and the flea. In the flea, they are almost married and the flea is their marriage bed, their "marriage temple." Although her parents are not agreeable to their union and she refuses to make love with him, they are, nevertheless, united in the body of the flea: "in these living walls of jet." The poet tells her that if she kills the flea, she will not only kill it but also him and her, so she will be committing three sins: "three sins in killing three." She eventually kills the flea with her fingernail, purpling it with the "blood of innocence." He tells her that she is "cruel" and asks her what wrong the flea had done to her except that she took a drop of her blood, "it suck'd from thee." She tells him that now she has killed the flea they are not any less noble, but he replies that, likewise, she would not be losing any less honor if she slept with him, "when thou yield'st to me" than when she killed the flea.

The poem narrates a story of seduction where the poet attempts to seduce his lover. The flea functions at first as a metaphor which unites the two lovers through the mingling of their blood. The flea is supposed to persuade the lover that they are already one and "married" in the flea, so the lover should have no fear of loss of honor. The woman, however, is not persuaded and kills the flea, squashing it under her nail. The killing of the flea, which amounts to the literalizing of the metaphor, puts an end to the figural meaning carried by the flea in the poem. However, the poem does not end here but gives way to its allegorical or didactic function. The death of the flea becomes the lesson that the poet wants to impart to his lover. The death of the flea demonstrates how false the woman's fears to lose her honor are. Just as the death of the flea has not made her weaker, so her fears of losing honor if she gives herself to him are unfounded: "Just so much honor, when thou yield'st to me,/ Will waste, as this flea's death took life from thee."

The conceit of the flea, which characterizes the poem, does not, in and of itself, explain the seduction that takes place in the poem. Rather, the flea is a vehicle for the poem's final allegorical or didactic function which is made possible by the disruption, or the "killing," of the metaphor of the flea. The conceit of the flea carries its traditional erotic connotations but it is only a means for the poem final syllogism, whose logic is meant to persuade the lover. The poem, which Dr. Johnson called metaphysical, is essentially prosaic or allegorical, or Baroque.

The Good Morrow

The next poem by Donne is "The Good Morrow" (Shawcross, 89), whose theme is still love, but the erotic aspect, which is in the foreground in "The Flea," is secondary here. The poem is as follows:

The Good Morrow

I wonder, by my troth, what thou and I
Did, till we loved? Were we not weaned till then?
But sucked on country pleasures, childishly?
Or snorted we in the Seven Sleepers' den?
'Twas so; but this, all pleasures fancies be.
If ever any beauty I did see,
Which I desired, and got, 'twas but a dream of thee.

And now good-morrow to our waking souls,
Which watch not one another out of fear;
For love, all love of other sights controls,
And makes one little room an everywhere.
Let sea-discoverers to new worlds have gone,
Let maps to other, worlds on worlds have shown,
Let us possess one world, each hath one, and is one.

My face in thine eye, thine in mine appears,
And true plain hearts do in the faces rest;
Where can we find two better hemispheres,
Without sharp north, without declining west?
Whatever dies, was not mixed equally;
If our two loves be one, or, thou and I
Love so alike, that none do slacken, none can die.

As the title indicates, the emphasis of the poem is on the "Good Morrow" and the realization of the meaning of their love when the poet and his lover wake up on the "good morrow." The poem is in the form of address in a language which is direct and colloquial. The poet asks his lover what they did before they fell in love, "what thou and I did, till we lov'd." Were they mere babies at their mothers' breasts, or indulging in childish "country pleasures," or perhaps they were asleep as in the Seven Sleepers' den? The latter is a reference to an ancient legend when persecuted Christians slept for several hundred years in a cave near Ephesus. When they woke up their world had changed and had become Christian. With these three questions, the nature and role of Love is emphasized and explained: 1) "were we not wean'd till then? 2) But suck'd on country pleasures, childishly?" 3) "Or snorted we in the Seven Sleepers' den?"

The first two questions are related: "not weaned" indicates the souls' lack of maturity and ignorance in their infancy before Love woke them up. Before they fell in love, they were like babies and indulged in childish "country pleasures." Both questions make strong allusions to sexual gratification. The third question "snort'd we in the Seven Sleepers' den" addresses the title directly: waking and sleeping. There is also, here, an implication of a miraculous sleep, compared to the sleep in the poem. The original legend of the seven sleepers is a reference to both the Christian and the Mohammedan religion at the dawn of Christianity, which Helen Gardner, in her co-edited work, *The Elegies and The Songs and Sonnets,* explains its importance in detail.[5]

The legend, according to the translation from the Syrian in *De Gloria Martyrum* by Gregory of Tours, relates that about AD 250 or 251, during the persecution of the Christians by the Emperor Decius, seven Christian youth from Ephesus took refuge in a cave in a nearby mountain. Their pursuers walled them in a cave, with the intention of starving them to death, but the young men fell into a miraculous sleep, from which they did not wake until some time during the reign of Theodosius II (possibly AD 439 or AD 446). When they woke up, they thought they had been asleep for only a single night, and one of them, who went to the city for food, was amazed to find, on churches and other buildings, the cross, which, when he had fallen asleep, had been an object of desecration. The legend has strong implications that devoutness brings miracles. This literary reference shows not only Donne's Roman Catholic background, but also the dawn of spirituality, as Bloom has suggested.[6]

The opposing concepts in the legend characterize the qualitative difference between before and after waking. First of all, the contrast between one night and two centuries, within which there are two possible levels of meaning: 1) one night could be as long as two centuries, during which things change: the dawning of the morning brings a new world. Christianity, in the legend, once the subject of hatred, is now believed and worshiped. 2) Two centuries could also be as short as one night. Things are unchanged, uninspired and unknown before waking up. One night here refers to the night the seven youths of Ephesus spent in the cave, and also the night the poet spent with his lover, which just passed. When the seven youths of Ephesus woke up, they found a new world dominated by the victory of their belief, Christianity; when the lovers wake up, the new world they find is the miraculous joy of Love which triumphs over sexual pleasure. The analogy emphasizes the unpredictability of the world as it changes in time and space, as the sense of time is uncertain and cannot be trusted. The seven youths of Ephesus felt that they had slept one single night, but the night turns out to be two centuries. Although the physical place does not change during their sleep, the spirituality of the outside world has been turned upside down, which is why the waking soul does not realize the change in spirituality until the morning after. Once the lovers wake up from their sleep, they question the time difference and the difference between the world before and after.

As the speaker wonders why they fell in love so late, the first four lines focus mainly on "sleeping" and its unconscious state – the time before they fell in Love. Before falling in love, the poet saw in ignorance, desired and got what he thought was beauty. But now that he has found his "true" love, he realizes that all his past pleasures, and the women he "desir'd," were merely "fancies," they were only a "dream" of this one woman he is in love in with, only "a dream of thee."

On the "good morrow" their souls wake up to a constant, trusting love. They do not need to keep a jealous eye on each other because their love subdues the desire to look for others. It is so complete, so self-sufficient, that it "makes one little room, an everywhere." In the next stanza, the emphasis moves to the external world which the lovers have abandoned for each other. There may be worlds out there: let discoverers go and find them, or map-makers draw them, the lovers will use their time taking possession of their own private world. This world is complete because it is made up of two hemispheres that perfectly complement each other. The poet also suggests that if their love is constant, they cannot die, since only what is contrary or of different measure can disintegrate. "If our two loves be one, or, thou and I/ Love so alike, that none do slacken, none can die." They will be able to live in perfect harmony.

The second stanza begins with a greeting to their "waking souls" as they awaken into a constant trusting love. Their waking souls look at each other not "out of fear" – as they have no need to fear that they may look for other partners. Their love controls sight; as sight is on each other, there is no space for other things, and the little room they are in is everywhere. They form one world and care only for one another. Let navigators find new continents and let the world expand and the rest of the people get to know the planet they live on. The lovers only want one spiritual world combined by two originally separated souls, similar to the two hemispheres of the planet which are explored by navigators and mappers. Each one is an independent world, and each of them has one world. As they are combined by Love, they become one in the one and only world they want to possess, to explore and discover more of each other, to merge completely and be one. Harold Bloom suggests "juxtaposition" to understand the two worlds each one has between the sensual and the spiritual world and concludes that "this juxtaposition of the sensual with the spiritual suggests that those who live solely in the sensual world, busying themselves in mundane matters, are lost to the world of true love" (Bloom 16).

In the third stanza, their love is attuned not only to physical appearances but also to their hearts: their eyes can see only their faces, and their sight can only see their true hearts. They want an ideal world all to themselves, without any shortcomings: a world without sharp north or declining west. As commentators suggest, the sharp north represents the coldness which may freeze the warmth of love and the declining west represents the sunset or the decay of the outside world. The last three lines deal with the immortality of love: "whatever dies, was not mix'd equally." Equality is extremely valued as the preventer of Death, but also an important factor which requires that their hemispheres be equal in every sense, including their geographical dimensions. When the lovers find their ideal world where they are equal, their love will not die. The poet now expresses the wish, which is the point of the poem: If "thou and I" really love each other, they will put equal effort in their united world, so that their love will not die and they, because of their everlasting love, will not die as well.

As in "The Flea," the poem is a discourse on love which takes its starting point from the legend of the Seven Sleepers to differentiate between erotic and spiritual, or "true" love. The "good morrow" is the diving line that allows for a radical shift in the lovers' new awareness of their love for one another. Characteristically, the ending of the poem sums up the lesson that the poet wants to impart: if the lovers are "one" and their "love" be "alike," then their love will never die. The final lines sum up the truth of the argument that the poet has been arguing throughout the poem: by leaving behind the erotic, true, spiritual life will consecrate their love, eternally. As in "The Flea" this poem is not a lyric, as Dr. Johnson claimed, but a piece of metaphysics, a discourse on love, prosaic or allegorical, or Baroque.

The Sun Rising

"For love ... makes one little room, an everywhere." This witty conceit appears again in "The Sun Rising," the third poem by John Donne I have chosen to discuss (Shawcross, 93):

The Sun Rising

Busy old fool, unruly sun,
Why dost thou thus,
Through windows, and through curtains call on us?
Must to thy motions lovers' seasons run?
Saucy pedantic wretch, go chide
Late school boys and sour prentices,
Go tell court huntsmen that the king will ride,
Call country ants to harvest offices,

Love, all alike, no season knows nor clime,
Nor hours, days, months, which are the rags of time.

Thy beams, so reverend and strong
Why shouldst thou think?
I could eclipse and cloud them with a wink,
But that I would not lose her sight so long;
If her eyes have not blinded thine,
Look, and tomorrow late, tell me,
Whether both th' Indias of spice and mine
Be where thou leftst them, or lie here with me.
Ask for those kings whom thou saw'st yesterday,
And thou shalt hear,
All here in one bed lay.

She's all states, and all princes, I,
Nothing else is.
Princes do but play us; compared to this,
All honor's mimic, all wealth alchemy.
Thou, sun, art half as happy as we,
In that the world's contracted thus.
Thine age asks ease, and since thy duties be
To warm the world, that's done in warming us.
Shine here to us, and thou art everywhere;
This bed thy center is, these walls, thy sphere.

Differently from the previous two poems which address his lover, in this poem, the dialogue is with the sun. The poet scolds the sun, calling it "busy old fool." His complaint against the sun is that when he rises, he wakes and disturbs him and his beloved from their sleep. The lovers' seasons do not change according to the sun but have their own pace, which is set by the lovers. The poet urges the sun to go and annoy schoolboys and rush them to school, or to call the huntsmen to prepare for the king's ride, or the farmer to work in the fields. The sun, which creates time, has no influence on love, and in love, there is no time: "Love, all alike, no season knows, nor clime, / Nor hours, days, months, which are the rags of time."

In the second stanza, the poet goes on mocking the sun: although the sun shines over the world, and its beams are very bright, they are not comparable to love's "brightness." The poet could easily deny the sun by closing his eyes, if he did not want to keep them always open to keep his beloved in sight. If he were only to wink, he would not be able to see his beloved and that moment is "so long." The poet boosts that his beloved's eyes shine much more bright than the sun and her beams would even blind the sun's eyes. In his praise of the beloved's beauty and loveliness, Donne employs a convention of the Renaissance love poem, but he masterly converts it into a hypothesis: "if her eyes have not blinded you," which makes the conceit much stronger and more convincing. If his beloved has not blinded him, can the sun tell him if all the treasures of India are still there or if they are in bed with him: "Whether both Indias, of spice and mine, / Be where thou leftst them, or lie here with me." The reference is to both the East and West Indies, which, in Donne's time, had become known for their spices and precious mines. The poet now claims that his beloved is all of those precious treasures of the East and West Indies, and they are in bed with him: "all here in one bed lay."

The poet explains that his beloved is equal to "all States," and he is "all Princes, I,/ Nothing else is." All the States belong to the prince and his beloved yields to him. Compared to the bond which unites the lovers, all honors and wealth of the world are not real, they are false. The poet mocks the sun who has to work hard to warm the outside world, but he offers him an alternative: to narrow the whole world down to the two of them and their room, and to the bed they are in: "To warm the world, that's done in warming us. / Shine here to us, and thou art everywhere; / This bed thy centre is, these walls, thy sphere."

In this third poem, the personification of the sun makes possible a wide variety of conceits typical of Donne's poems: the conceit that love overcomes time: "no season knows, nor clime, / Nor hours, days, months, which are the rags of time"; that only the sphere of love matters, while the physical and real worlds are easily dispensable. At the end, he can claim that their bedroom is the whole world and their bed its center. While "The Flea" is about seduction and the "Good Morrow" about the overcoming of the erotic in the spiritual, this third poem is basically a rhetorical "tour de force" with all the clichés that have come to be associated with Donne's poetry. There are no lessons to be learned at the end of this rhetorical exercise but, in typically Baroque fashion, the poem demonstrates Donne's rhetorical ability, and includes him in the long list of his Western Baroque counterparts that specialized in "wonder" (maraviglia).[7]

Andrew Marvell: *Eros* and *Thanatos*

Andrew Marvell is perhaps the other most important metaphysical poet. As Jack Dalglish writes, his work "reveals the successful assimilation and fusion of the two great poetic influences of the early seventeenth century: it combines the passionate, probing intellectuality of Donne with the clarity and poise of Johnson."[8] Marvell is best at handling verses of intense emotions, sometimes expressing seriousness through wit and irony, or relating trivial thoughts as profoundly important issues. Nigel Smith, the editor of *The Poems of Andrew Marvell*, comments that his poems "reflect deeply on the nature of poetry, ancient and modern, classical, Renaissance and contemporary, European and English. He thought about the identity of the poet and his responsibilities to public and private realms."[9] Marvell's poetry confronts two basic problems facing the poet writing in the seventeenth century: on the one hand, the relationship between amorous and devotional verse and, on the other, the challenge to fixed beliefs represented by the world of public life and politics. The three poems selected here are on the theme of love: "To His Coy Mistress," "The Definition of Love" and "The Unfortunate Lovers."

To his Coy Mistress

The poem "To His Coy Mistress" follows a long tradition of classic and Renaissance love poetry that was written around the motif of *carpe diem*, which is to urge the beloved to "seize the day" and enjoy love, usually sex, before it is too late and death overtakes the lovers. "To His Coy Mistress" is probably the best-known poem of Andrew Marvell and one of the most famous *carpe diem* poems in English. The poet addresses his mistress to persuade her to give herself to him. The persuasion involves clever allusions, witticisms and conceits in a clever and well-structured framework. The poem unfolds in a monologue tone and the argument is developed logically in three stages to persuade his mistress that life is short, and they better enjoy love before they die.

To His Coy Mistress[10]

Had we but world enough and time,
This coyness, lady, were no crime.
We would sit down, and think which way
To walk, and pass our long love's day.
Thou by the Indian Ganges' side
Shouldst rubies find; I by the tide
Of Humber would complain. I would
Love you ten years before the flood,
And you should, if you please, refuse
Till the conversion of the Jews.
My vegetable love should grow
Vaster than empires and more slow;
An hundred years should go to praise
Thine eyes, and on thy forehead gaze;
Two hundred to adore each breast,
But thirty thousand to the rest;
An age at least to every part,

And the last age should show your heart.
For, lady, you deserve this state,
Nor would I love at lower rate.

But at my back I always hear
Time's wingèd chariot hurrying near;
And yonder all before us lie
Deserts of vast eternity.
Thy beauty shall no more be found;
Nor, in thy marble vault, shall sound
My echoing song; then worms shall try
That long-preserved virginity,
And your quaint honour turn to dust,
And into ashes all my lust;
The grave's a fine and private place,
But none, I think, do there embrace.

Now therefore, while the youthful hue
Sits on thy skin like morning dew,
And while thy willing soul transpires
At every pore with instant fires,
Now let us sport us while we may,
And now, like amorous birds of prey,
Rather at once our time devour
Than languish in his slow-chapped power.
Let us roll all our strength and all
Our sweetness up into one ball,
And tear our pleasures with rough strife
Through the iron gates of life:
Thus, though we cannot make our sun
Stand still, yet we will make him run.

The poet tries to persuade his mistress to give herself to him. If they had all the time in the world, there would be time to enjoy each other but since there is little precious time, they should not be wasting it. The poet makes use of the millenarian ideas of the seventeenth century, biblical references and the concept of the tripartite soul, to exaggerate the idea of time. "I would/ Love you ten years before the flood: / And you should, if you please, refuse / Till the conversation of the Jews." The Flood is recorded in the Old Testament and refers to God's decision to return to earth, following the "conversion of the Jews," and the second coming of Christ. The poet uses these ideas to express the length of time that would take his shy mistress who hesitates. The reference to "vegetable love" is to the "vegetable" soul, which, according to Aristotle, is the basic soul, and describes the love of the poet, which is basic and instinctive, and grows vastly and slowly. It would take a hundred years to see and praise the mistress' eyes and forehead, two hundred years for each breast; in short, it would take thirty thousand years to praise every part of her body: "An age at least to every part, / And the last age should show your heart." His mistress deserves all this time and all his intense love, however, there is not enough time in this world for him to love her properly: "Had we but world enough, and time."

The poet continues his argument by impressing upon his mistress that they are just finite human beings and they should take advantage of their bodies while they are youthful, "Now let us sport us while we may"; before her beauty will perish, "Thy beauty shall no more be found"; and the virginity she wants to preserve will be left to the worms, after she is dead. When she dies, her virgin honor will turn to dust, as will her body and virginity, and the poet's body will turn to ashes as well. Although the grave is a fine and a private place for lovers to meet, those who lie in graves will never be able to embrace their lovers. Although Marvell is using images of death and decay that are typical of *carpe diem* lyrics, his images are more graphic when he describes that only worms will enjoy her virginity: "in thy marble vault . . . / worms shall try/ That long-preserved virginity:/ And your quaint honor turn to dust."

In the last stanza, the poet sums up his argument by trying to convince his mistress to take action. They should take advantage of the fact that they are still young and desirable; they should love each other while they can. In doing so, they can win a battle over the destructiveness of Time: "Thus, though we cannot make our sun/ Stand still, yet we will make him run." The imagery Marvell uses has always been a topic of controversy as his image of the lovers as "amorous birds of prey" is not felt to be very romantic and not what would make his mistress give in. "Let us . . . / Tear our pleasures with rough strife/ Thorough the iron grates of life." Some commentators have felt that Love is not described as being "conventionally sweet and sentimental but rather vaguely dangerous and threatening; beneath the surface, Marvell seems to be issuing a warning as much as an exhortation" (Nigel vii). However, it has also been suggested that the physicality of their encounter will not only bring them pleasure but will also bring them back to life. The gate of life can be seen as a witty take on the gate of death, a reversal of the imagery of the grave into the life that their sexual intimacy will bring them. This is the way the lovers will be able to enjoy (their) Time: "Thus, though we cannot make our sun / Stand still, yet we will make him run."

One difference between Donne and Marvell is that in Donne, love has power over time and death: "Love, all alike, no season knows, nor clime, / Nor hours, days, months, which are the rags of time." In Marvell, however, the poet is more aware that "we cannot make our sun"; the lovers will not be able to change time, but they will make good use of it: "yet we will make him run." "To His Coy Mistress," as a seduction poem is comparable to Donne's "The Flea" with the exception that while Donne's poem, as we have seen argues for why the lover should consent to the poet's advances, in Marvell's poem the attempt at seduction appears to take second place to the rhetorical bravado the poet uses to persuade his lover. This aspect of "To His Coy Mistress" is similar to Donne's "The Sun Rising": a rhetorical pyrotechnic for its own sake in the style of the best European Baroque. The darker aspects of the poet's arguments undermine the tradition of a love elegy, where the speaker praises his mistress through the motif of *carpe diem*, but they also subvert the pattern of Petrarchan love poetry, typical of the fifteenth and sixteenth centuries. Unlike Donne, Marvell does not structure his poem on logical arguments. As Nigel puts it, they seem to be "issuing a warning as much as an exhortation" (Nigel vii). Despite being one of the most well-known poems by Marvell, and the most Baroque, it is not the most typical of his poetic production.

The Definition of Love

"The Definition of Love" (Smith 107), the next poem I discuss is more typical of Andrew Marvell. The poem is comparable to Donne's "Good Morrow" because of its intensively elaborated imagery and neo-platonic implications of love, namely, that love of the soul is distinct from the love of the body. Differently from Donne's poem where the overcoming of the physical unites the lovers even more, in Marvell's poem perfection in love implies the impossibility of love. Rather than the fulfillment of love through union, as we have in Donne, the end result is the unattainability of love: "two perfect but irreconcilable" loves. Marvell subverts the traditional description of the process of love, "where hope usually precedes despair in descriptions of the progress of love" (Smith 107). In this poem, Love is generated by Despair because of its Impossibility:

The Definition of Love

Love is of a birth as rare
As 'tis for object strange and high;
It was begotten by Despair
Upon Impossibility.

Magnanimous Despair alone
Could show me so divine a thing
Where feeble Hope could ne'er have flown,
But vainly flapp'd its tinsel wing.

And yet I quickly might arrive
Where my extended soul is fixt,
But Fate does iron wedges drive,
And always crowds itself betwixt.

For Fate with jealous eye does see
Two perfect loves, nor lets them close;
Their union would her ruin be,
And her tyrannic pow'r depose.

And therefore her decrees of steel
Us as the distant poles have plac'd,
(Though love's whole world on us doth wheel)
Not by themselves to be embrac'd;

Unless the giddy heaven fall,
And earth some new convulsion tear;
And, us to join, the world should all
Be cramp'd into a planisphere.

As lines, so loves oblique may well
Themselves in every angle greet;
But ours so truly parallel,
Though infinite, can never meet.

Therefore the love which us doth bind,
But Fate so enviously debars,
Is the conjunction of the mind,
And opposition of the stars.

The poet defines love as being "rare" because it is the product of "Despair" and "Impossibility." Only the selfless and generous Despair could bring him such divine love. Hope could not have done that since it may prove itself ineffective and helpless because this love can never be achieved. He could have easily obtained it except that Fate intervened and thwarted his hopes: "But Fate does iron wedges drive, / And always crowds itself betwixt." Fate is jealous of perfect Love and conspires to separate the lovers: "Two perfect loves" and Fate will not allow them to come together, "nor lets them close." Their perfect union would be the ruin of Fate, which does not allow happiness, which would diminish her power: "And her tyrannic pow'r depose."

The rest of the poem is taken up with a discussion of Fate and how it places the lovers in two separate spheres, poles apart, so that they will never be able to be united. Fate's decree makes it impossible for the lovers to ever meet, both physically and spiritually. Although the planet goes around, the perfect lovers never have the possibility to embrace each other on their own power. The symbols of iron wedges and steel decrees suggest that Fate has dominion over the world but also over the physical bodies of the lovers. The only possibility for them to be united is if heaven were to fall, earth collapse, and the planet were to be compressed "into a planisphere," that is, never.

The poet compares the two lovers to two infinite lines that together make a perfect circle, but since the lines are parallel they will never meet: "But ours so truly parallel, / Though infinite, can never meet." Here the geometric conceit is employed to oppose the two perfect lovers with common lovers, and to emphasize the impossibility of their ever coming together. The common lovers are like oblique lines; they meet because their nature is less perfect; the two perfect lovers, instead, are parallel lines, they extend to infinity and never meet because they are perfect.

The poet blames Fate for keeping the lovers apart. What Love wills them together, Fate will keep apart: "Therefore the love which us doth bind,/ But Fate so enviously debars." What is left to the two lovers, who are denied physical union, and what diminishes their despair, is their "union of minds": "the conjunction of the mind, / And opposition of the stars." This conclusion contrasts with the ending of "To His Coy Mistress." While in this poem the poet is still able to persuade his lover to give herself to him, in this poem the poet has lost all hope, and all that he can offer her is to accept a platonic relationship, a "union of minds."

The Unfortunate Lover

The next poem by Marvell, "The Unfortunate Lover" (Smith, 85) is very much in this negative vein. The definition of love as "despair" results logically in "The Unfortunate Lover" who is continuously defeated by the designs of Fate. The lovers always move parallel to each other but they never meet. Their destiny is to be only lovers of the mind but not of the body.

The Unfortunate Lover

Alas, how pleasant are their days
With whom the infant Love yet plays!
Sorted by pairs, they still are seen
By fountains cool, and shadows green.
But soon these flames do lose their light,
Like meteors of a summer's night:

Nor can they to that region climb,
To make impression upon time.

'Twas in a shipwreck, when the seas
Ruled, and the winds did what they please,
That my poor lover floating lay,
And, ere brought forth, was cast away:
Till at the last the master-wave
Upon the rock his mother grave;
And there she split against the stone,
In a Caesarean sectión.

The sea him lent those bitter tears
Which at his eyes he always wears;
And from the winds the sighs he bore,
Which through his surging breast do roar.
No day he saw but that which breaks
Through frighte'd clouds in forkèd streaks,
While round the rattling thunder hurled,
As at the funeral of the world.

While Nature to his birth presents
This masque of quarrelling elements,
A numerous fleet of cormorants black,
That sailed insulting o'er the wrack,
Received into their cruel care
Th' unfortunate and abject heir:
Guardians most fit to entertain
The orphan of the hurricane.

They fed him up with hopes and air,
Which soon digested to despair,
And as one cormorant fed him, still
Another on his heart did bill,
Thus while they famish him, and feast,
He both consumèd, and increased:
And languishèd with doubtful breath,
The amphibíum of life and death.

And now, when angry heaven would
Behold a spectacle of blood,
Fortune and he are called to play

At sharp before it all the day:
And tyrant Love his breast does ply
With all his winged artillery,
Whilst he, betwixt the flames and waves,
Like Ajax, the mad tempest braves.

See how he nak'd and fierce does stand,
Cuffing the thunder with one hand,
While with the other he does lock,
And grapple, with the stubborn rock:
From which he with each wave rebounds,
Torn into flames, and ragg'd with wounds,
And all he 'says, a lover dressed
In his own blood does relish best.

This is the only banneret
That ever Love created yet:
Who though, by the malignant stars,
Forcèd to live in storms and wars,
Yet dying leaves a perfume here,
And music within every ear:
And he in story only rules,
In a field sable a lover gules.

The poem narrates the tragic story of the unfortunate lover's life from before his birth to his death. His story begins with the Infant Love who spends his pleasant days by streams and shades but his love does not last: "Alas, how pleasant are their days / With whom the infant Love yet plays!" His love is like a meteor which vanishes suddenly and leaves no trace in time. His birth is tragic. It happens in a shipwreck when his mother, in collision with a rock, gives birth to him. The unfortunate lover is born as a result of the impact and he comes into this world with a "Caesarean section." This is the beginning of his unfortunate life and the sea provides him with the "bitter tears," which accompany him throughout his life.

The next stanzas narrate his upbringing: how he was the heir of an estate but fell unfortunately in the "cruel care" of greedy guardians who fed him with both hope and despair: "They fed him up with hopes and air, / which soon digested to despair." They exploited him and took advantage of him: "as one cormorant fed him, still / Another on his heart did bill." As a result, he became weaker and feebler living in an environment which prepared him both for life and death: "Th' amphibium of Life and Death."

In the next sixth and seven stanzas, the poet describes the continued misfortunes of the unfortunate lover. Fortune seems dead set against him and even Heaven is "angry" at him, and seems to enjoy a "spectacle of blood." When Love becomes concerned with him and shoots him with its arrows of desire, he lost hope that his love could be fulfilled. He was like Ajax, the son of Oileus, who had to brave "the mad tempest." Now he was facing three attacks – from the flames of love, from the waves of Fortune, and from the mad tempest. The last two refer to his other misfortunes and to how he was exploited by his greedy guardians. As a lover, he tried in vain to fight against Fate. He fought these unequal fights bravely, "cuffing the thunder with one hand," and the rock with the other, but he is torn into flames, and "ragg'd with wounds." Only a lover who has gone through a similar experience can understand his feelings: "he says: a lover dressed/ In his own blood does relish best."

However, there seems to be some consolation for the unfortunate lover. In the last stanza, we are told that at his death, the unfortunate lover's name will be praised and he will be remembered and his memory cherished. He leaves behind fame and glory, and his story will be put to music and played for generations to come. He becomes a hero and his image will be colored with the red of his blood. As in the previous poem, the consolation for the unfortunate lover is that his name will be remembered and he will be rewarded with fame and glory.

An interesting reading of the "Unfortunate Lover" comes from Hirst and Zwicker who make the case for "The Unfortunate Lover" as the supreme text of the poet's imagined life, and as the key to understanding his whole poetic production.[11] In their view, the poem exemplifies the contrast between a diversified poetry and an obscure biography, and the ambiguities and contradictions they generate. For instance, they find "shocking" that a poem of seduction such as "To his Coy Mistress," despite "its simulacrum of heterosexual ecstasy," actually suggests "misogyny and [heterosexual] aversion" when "worms and decay" serve as the prompt to desire" (Hirst 386). A similar fear of annihilation in heterosexuality shapes the argument of the "Unfortunate Lover" (Hirst 387).

The "Unfortunate Lover," to a great extent, explains these contradictions since it is a narrative of the self in the world, which narrates the Unfortunate Lover's traumatic experience, from a Caesarian birth, "as descent in a world of dissonance and differentiation" (Hirst 374), to the death of his father by drowning (Hirst 375), and the (erotic) abuse from the cormorants, a figure of rapacity which parallels the "tyrannical and voracious, abusive and wounding" behavior of the clergy in their black robes (a possible reference to the religious struggles of 1640) (Hirst 375). This is a form of sexual abuse that the authors suggest was done with "the availability of the child to erotic attachment" (Hirst

376). However, at the end of this narrative of trauma and suffering, it is imagination which triumphs, and this poem, as well as Marvell's poetry in general, are evidence of this triumph. Eternity, the authors conclude, is only to be possessed through verse, which is the conclusion of all Marvell's poems. "Here [in "The Unfortunate Lover"] is a model of the writing life; here is a natural history of the imagination written out … as the biography of the Unfortunate Lover" (Hirst 379).

Andrew Marvell's poetry became available to the public well after his death. The poet had kept his poetry unpublished until then. Perhaps Hirst and Zwicker are correct in their analysis: his poetry became more and more autobiographical and less and less Baroque, although it did not lose its prosaic or allegorical style.

Richard Crashaw: Eros and Ecstasy

Crashaw is known for the vibrant stylistic ornamentation of his verses. As he was highly influenced by seventeenth-century Spanish and Italian poetry, he reflected little of his contemporary English metaphysical poets, but, instead, he adhered to the highly emotional and ornate imagery of the continental Baroque poets. He used conceits to draw analogies between the physical beauties of nature and the spiritual significance of existence. His verse is marked by loose trains of association, sensuous imagery, and eager religious emotion. One of his methods of conveying the intensity of his religious feelings is the use of erotic language, a technique which he probably learned from Donne, although, according to Itrat-Husain, the Catholic mind tends to use "a sensuous vehicle to express spiritual states and tries to interpret the invisible with the help of the visible, hence the frequent use of erotic symbolism in the Roman Catholic mysticism."[12] The erotic imagery of "To the Noblest and Best of Ladies, The Countess of Denbigh,"[13] which is the first poem by Crashaw I examine, are those that are typically used in the "parody of seduction poetry."

To The Noblest and Best of Ladies,
the Countess of Denbigh[14]

What Heaven-entreated heart is this,
Stands trembling at the gate of bliss?
Holds fast the door, yet dares not venture
Fairly to open it, and enter;
Whose definition is a doubt
'Twixt life and death, 'twixt in and out.
Say, lingering fair, why comes the birth

Of your brave soul so slowly forth?
Plead your pretenses, O you strong
In weakness, why you choose so long
In labor of yourself to lie,
Not daring quite to live nor die.
Ah, linger not, loved soul! A slow
And late consent was a long no;
Who grants at last, long time tried
And did his best to have denied.
What magic bolts, what mystic bars
Maintain the will in these strange wars!
What fatal, yet fantastic bands
Keep the free heart from its own hands!
So when the year takes cold we see
Poor waters their own prisoners be;
Fettered and locked up fast they lie
In a sad self-captivity.
The astonished nymphs their flood's strange fate deplore,
To see themselves their own severer shore.
Thou that alone canst thaw this cold,
And fetch the heart from its stronghold,
Almighty Love! end this long war,
And of a meteor make a star.
Oh, fix this fair indefinite,
And 'mongst Thy shafts of sovereign light
Choose out that sure decisive dart
Which has the key of this close heart,
Knows all the corners of 't, and can control
The self-shut cabinet of an unsearched soul.
Oh, let it be at last Love's hour;
Raise this tall trophy of Thy power;
Come once the conquering way, not to confute
But kill this rebel-word, 'irresolute,'
That so, in spite of all this peevish strength
Of weakness, she may write, 'Resolved at length.'
Unfold at length, unfold, fair flower,
And use the season of Love's shower;
Meet His well-meaning wounds, wise heart!
And haste to drink the wholesome dart,
That healing shaft, which Heaven till now
Hath in Love's quiver hid for you.

O dart of Love! arrow of light!
O happy you, if it hit right!
It must not fall in vain, it must
Not mark the dry regardless dust.
Fair one, it is your fate, and brings
Eternal worlds upon its wings.
Meet it with wide-spread arms, and see
Its seat your soul's just center be.
Disband dull fears, give faith the day;
To save your life, kill your delay.
It is Love's siege, and sure to be
Your triumph, through His victory.
'Tis cowardice that keeps this field,
And want of courage not to yield.
Yield then, O yield, that Love may win
The fort at last, and let life in;
Yield quickly, lest perhaps you prove
Death's prey, before the prize of Love.
This fort of your fair self, if't be not won,
He is repulsed indeed, but you're undone.

The Countess was the widow of the Earl of Denbigh, who died in 1643, fighting for King Charles I. She was a lady-in-waiting to Charles I's Catholic Queen Henrietta Maria. When the Queen fled to Paris to avoid the Civil War, the Countess followed her in exile. She was not Catholic and had not fully committed to Roman Catholicism until she met Crashaw in Paris and considered converting. He wrote this poem to persuade her and he succeeded.

The poet does not attempt to convert her to the new religion. He does not use theological arguments, and he does not once refer to the Catholic Church. Even God is not referred to directly except as "Allmighty Love." The poem is about resolution, about making a difficult decision. The poem addresses the Countess's heart, depicting it as terrified and irresolute, standing on the threshold, daring not to accept what the poet believes to be the one true faith: "trembling at the gate of bliss; / Holds fast the door, ye dares not venture/ Fairly to open it, and enter." The conceits he employs deal with birth and delivery. The main section of the poem deals with the conceit of being "in labor of yourself," in the sense that only her willfulness can deliver her soul: "why come the birth of your brave soul so slowly forth?" The poet questions her indecision, her hesitation not daring to choose, and lying to herself: "O you strong/ In weakness, why you choose so long/ In labor of yourself to lie, Not daring quite to live nor die." He brings up the image of consent, as in a marriage proposal, when delaying too long implies "a long no": "a slow/ And late consent was a long no." Delaying a decision can be fatal, "fatal bands," causing paralysis of the will.

Crashaw employs the door metaphor to depict the heart and the ideological struggle of the Countess: "What magic bolts, what magic bars / maintain the will in these strange wars." He makes use of paradox to express concepts that are otherwise quite conventional in a religious context, for instance, the notion of keeping her heart free, "open" to choices, which actually binds it. The reference to wars, as in "these strange warres," although it may be a reference to the Civil War going on in England, it also refers, in this context, to her psychological and spiritual "war." The image, which compares the Countess, "frozen" in her irresolution, is that of water frozen by the winter cold, which holds the waters in bondage: "Poor waters their own prisoners be/ Fettered, and locked up fast they lie/ In a sad self-captivity." Man or woman, are not always aware of the forces that cause them to delay and to procrastinate, instead, believing they are still free to choose, they are actually "frozen" in their irresolution. They deplore their fate when, in fact, they are the only ones who can "thaw" their situation: "Thou that alone canst thaw this cold/ And fetch the heart from its stronghold."

Lines 29 to 43 shift the attention to "God," who is only named indirectly as the "Almighty Love!" to appeal to Him to solve this "war," this bind at the heart of the Countess, to "end this long war/ And of a meteor make a star." The poem becomes a prayer to the Almighty who knows all the corners of her soul and can unlock her heart: "The self-shut cabinet of an unsearched soul." It is also an appeal to the Countess to let it soon be the hour when God's love will triumph: "Oh, let it be at last Love's hour." The Countess is described as a "fair flower" and Cupid's arrows of love become those of God and are healing wounds, "his well-meaning wounds." The only enemy in this "war" is death, so the poet urges her to decide soon, before death comes:

> Yield then, O yield, that Love may win
> The fort at last, and let life in;
> Yield quickly, lest perhaps you prove
> Death's prey, before the prize of Love.
> This fort of your fair self, if't be not won,
> He is repulsed indeed, but you're undone.

The heart of the Countess may not obtain the prize of Love if death comes before she yields to God, the Almighty Love! However, death becomes the assistant of love when fate forces the lovers to die in another poem, "An Epitaph upon Husband and Wife, who died and were buried together" (Williams, 478).

An epitaph upon husband and wife.

Who died and were buried together.

To these whom death again did wed,
This grave's the second marriage-bed.
For though the hand of Fate could force
'Twixt soul and body a divorce,
It could not sever man and wife,
Because they both lived but one life.
Peace, good reader, do not weep;
Peace, the lovers are asleep.
They, sweet turtles, folded lie
In the last knot that love could tie.
Let them sleep, let them sleep on,
Till the stormy night be gone,
And the eternal morrow dawn;
Then the curtains will be drawn,
And they wake into a light
Whose day shall never die in night.

Their death is their second wedding and Death is the host at the ceremony. The grave becomes their second marriage bed to enjoy the love which will bind them together forever. Fate may force the lovers to die physically by separating their bodies and souls, but it could not deny their marriage because the lovers took vows before God and lived together in "one life." The poet tells us that it is sad to see the lovers die and to read of such pathos, but one should not weep, because their souls are not dead; they have just fallen asleep. The lovers are like turtles covered in their shells lying together sleeping in the same grave: this is the last bond with which love can bind these two souls. Although the grave is not comfortable, the stone pillow hard and the sheets are cold, it is safe because "love made the bed" for them. When the stormy night ends and the pathos is gone, eternal life will come. Then husband and wife will awake and rise from their dark grave to the heaven where there is no night, there is no death.

Although this short poem is written in a simple language, it is representative of most of Crashaw's themes: personified death, fate and love; the conceit of death as the second marriage, the grave as the marriage bed; the dualism of body and soul; the attempt to emotionally involve the reader, and, finally, the belief in eternal life after death.

Although Crashaw's poems are those of a devotional poet, there is no attempt to be doctrinal or to convert the reader. As Husain suggests, "his faith is nothing but the 'progressive fructification of dogma' in his soul; and it is love which helps the 'seeds of life' to blossom forth" (Husain 179). This love which becomes the symbol of faith is sensual love. Conversion to Roman Catholicism takes the form of yielding to almighty Love, to God, but always with erotic implications as at the end of "The Countess of Denbigh": "It is love's siege, and sure to be/ Your triumph, though his victory" (lines 59-60); "O yield, that love may win/ The fort at last, and let life in" (lines 63-4). This erotic love reappears as the mysterious joys of love in another poem, "The Flaming Heart" (Williams, 61).

The Flaming Heart

Well meaning readers! you that come as friends
And catch the precious name this piece pretends;
Make not too much hast to' admire
That fair-cheek't fallacy of fire.
That is a Seraphim, they say
And this the great Teresa.
Readers, be rul'd by me; and make
Here a well-plac't and wise mistake.
You must transpose the picture quite,
And spell it wrong to read it right;
Read Him for her, and her for him;
And call the Saint the Seraphim.
Painter, what didst thou understand
To put her dart into his hand!
See, even the yeares and size of him
Showes this the mother Seraphim.
This is the mistresse flame; and duteous he
Her happy fire-works, here, comes down to see.
O most poor-spirited of men!
Had thy cold Pencil kist her Pen
Thou couldst not so unkindly err
To show us This faint shade for Her.
Why man, this speakes pure mortall frame;
And mockes with female Frost love's manly flame.
One would suspect thou meant'st to print
Some weak, inferiour, woman saint.
But had thy pale-fac't purple took
Fire from the burning cheeks of that bright Booke
Thou wouldst on her have heap't up all
That could be found Seraphicall;

What e're this youth of fire weares fair,
Rosy fingers, radiant hair,
Glowing cheek, and glistering wings,
All those fair and flagrant things,
But before all, that fiery Dart
Had fill'd the Hand of this great Heart.
  Doe then as equall right requires,
Since His the blushes be, and her's the fires,
Resume and rectify thy rude design;
Undresse thy Seraphim into Mine.
Redeem this injury of thy art;
Give Him the vail, give her the dart.
  Give Him the vail; that he may cover
The Red cheeks of a rivall'd lover.
Asham'd that our world, now, can show
Nests of new Seraphims here below.
  Give her the Dart for it is she
(Fair youth) shootes both thy shaft and Thee
Say, all ye wise and well-peirc't hearts
That live and dy amidst her darts,
What is't your tastfull spirits doe prove
In that rare life of Her, and love?
Say and bear wittnes. Sends she not
A Seraphim at every shott?
What magazins of immortall Armes there shine!
Heavn's great artillery in each love-spun line.
Give then the dart to her who gives the flame;
Give him the veil, who gives the shame.
  But if it be the frequent fate
Of worst faults to be fortunate;
If all's præscription; and proud wrong
Hearkens not to an humble song;
For all the gallantry of him,
Give me the suffring Seraphim.
His be the bravery of all those Bright things.
The glowing cheekes, the glistering wings;
The Rosy hand, the radiant Dart;
Leave Her alone The Flaming Heart.
  Leave her that; and thou shalt leave her
Not one loose shaft but love's whole quiver.
For in love's feild was never found

A nobler weapon then a Wound.
Love's passives are his activ'st part.
The wounded is the wounding heart.
O Heart! the æquall poise of love's both parts
Bigge alike with wound and darts.
Live in these conquering leaves; live all the same;
And walk through all tongues one triumphant Flame.
Live here, great Heart; and love and dy and kill;
And bleed and wound; and yeild and conquer still.
Let this immortall life wherere it comes
Walk in a crowd of loves and Martyrdomes
Let mystick Deaths wait on't; and wise soules be
The love-slain wittnesses of this life of thee.
O sweet incendiary! shew here thy art,
Upon this carcasse of a hard, cold, hart,
Let all thy scatter'd shafts of light, that play
Among the leaves of thy larg Books of day,
Combin'd against this Brest at once break in
And take away from me my self and sin,
This gratious Robbery shall thy bounty be;
And my best fortunes such fair spoiles of me.
O thou undanted daughter of desires!
By all thy dowr of Lights and Fires;
By all the eagle in thee, all the dove;
By all thy lives and deaths of love;
By thy larg draughts of intellectuall day,
And by thy thirsts of love more large then they;
By all thy brim-fill'd Bowles of feirce desire
By thy last Morning's draught of liquid fire;
By the full kingdome of that finall kisse
That seiz'd thy parting Soul, and seal'd thee his;
By all the heav'ns thou hast in him
(Fair sister of the Seraphim!)
By all of Him we have in Thee;
Leave nothing of my Self in me.
Let me so read thy life, that I
Unto all life of mine may dy.

The poem is best understood as an example of the differences between a symbolic and an allegorical reading. Unlike the previous two poems, this one invites the direct participation of the reader. "The Flaming Heart" is a poem about Saint Teresa of Avila and is the third poem of a trilogy.[15] As the full title indicates, "The Flaming Heart upon the Book and Picture of the Seraphicall Saint Teresa (as She is Usually Expressed with a Seraphim beside her)," the poem is based on a painting of the Saint which, in turn, was based on her autobiography. The main focus of the poem, however, is not the Saint herself but how she is portrayed by the painter or, better, how the painter misrepresents her in his painting. Crashaw's aim in the poem is to redress the errors of the painter and to provide the readers with a true picture of the events of her martyrdom. He hopes that readers, when viewing the painting, will be able to read it correctly.

> Well-meaning readers! you that come as freinds
> And catch the pretious name this piece pretends;
> Make not too much hast to' admire
> That fair-cheek't fallacy of fire.
> That is a Seraphim, they say
> And this the great Tereisa.
> Readers, be rul'd by me; and make
> Here a well-plac't and wise mistake.
> You must transpose the picture quite,
> And spell it wrong to read it right;

The poet asks for his readers' full attention, "be rul'd by me," so that they are not misled by the painting of Saint Teresa and the seraph. He asks them to make a "wise mistake" and switch Teresa with the seraph, and read him for her: "Read Him for her, and her for him;/ And call the Saint the Seraphim." [Seraphim is the plural of seraph and Crashaw is probably using it for the rhyme.] The painter misunderstood the events of her martyrdom and placed the dart in the seraph's hand, "Painter, what didst thou understand/ To put her dart into his hand!" The dart, instead, belongs to Saint Teresa, "the mistresse flame." The painter, being a poor-spirited man ("O most poor-spirited of men!"), was unkind to the Saint and depicted her as a pale and passive feminine figure, "To show us This faint shade for Her... Some weak, inferiour, woman saint." On the other hand, the painter gave the seraph all the alluring qualities, which he should have given the Saint. She deserves "the radiant hair, Glowing cheeks and glistering wings,/ All those fair and flagrant things," which the painter gave the seraph. He calls on the painter to rectify his mistake, and give the "blushes" to the seraph and the fire to Teresa:

Doe then as equall right requires,
Since His the blushes be, and her's the fires,
Resume and rectify thy rude design;

He tells the painter to "undress" his Seraph and suit him as he demands, and most of all, to give the seraph the veil, and the dart to Saint Teresa:

Undresse thy Seraphim into Mine.
Redeem this injury of thy art;
Give Him the vail, give her the dart.

The dart belongs to Teresa so she can pierce the hearts of men:

Give her the Dart for it is she
(Fair youth) shootes both thy shaft and Thee
Say, all ye wise and well-peirc't hearts
That live and dy amidst her darts.

The dart belongs to her who is the flame, while the veil belongs to the seraph for shame:

Give then the dart to her who gives the flame;
Give him the veil, who gives the shame.

If the painting cannot be changed, the poet is content to leave the dart to the seraph but the "Flaming Heart" is the Saint's alone: "Leave Her alone The Flaming Heart." The wounded heart is a more powerful weapon than the dart: "Leave her that; and thou shalt leave her/ Not one loose shaft but love's whole quiver./ For in love's field was never found/ A nobler weapon then a Wound." This is the conceit of the wound of love, which the Saint describes in her autobiography, *The Life of Saint Teresa of Jesus*: "another prayer very common is a certain kind of wounding; … but the suffering is so sweet, that one wishes it never would end."[16] This is the wound of love that Saint Teresa describes as the active and passive aspects of love: "O Heart! The aequall poise of love's both parts/ Bigge alike with wound and darts." Suffering is both active and passive love, and the truth which wounds others is the wounded heart itself: "Love's passives are his activ'st part/The wounded is the wounding heart." The saint's progress to martyrdom reaches its climax when the "mystick Deaths," and the "love-slain" witnesses appear.

In the last part of the poem, which was added later, the poet addresses Saint Teresa directly, not as she is portrayed in the painting but how she is in her autobiography, asking her to "wound" his hard and cold heart, "O sweet incendiary! shew thy art,/Upon this carcass of a hard, cold, hart." He appeals to her to "scatter all her "shafts of light" on him. He exhorts her to pierce him and relieve him of his sins and his self, "And take away from me my self and sin." The poem takes the form of a litany, an invocation by anaphora, to all things that are most sacred, beginning with "By all," "O thou undaunted daughter of desires!/ By all the dowr of Lights and Fires;/ By all the eagle...By all thy lives...By thy larg draughts... And by thy thirsts of love...By all thy brim-fill'd Bowles...By thy last Morning's draught... By the full kingdome...By all the heav'ns thou hast in him." He addresses the Saint as "Fair sister of the Seraphim!" and asks her, by all the power of the divinity invested in her, to possess him and convert him by taking his self away, "Leave nothing of my Self in me."

The "conversion" the poet asks is through the medium of the book. By reading her book he hopes to be be converted, "Let me so read thy life, that I/ Unto all life of mine may dy." Although Crashaw by the time he wrote the Trilogy on Saint Teresa (1646-1652)[17] he had already converted to Catholicism (around 1644), there is no indication that he was influenced by Saint Augustine whose conversion was made possible by reading the book of Scripture. Augustine heard an angel who told him to take the book and read it ("*tolle lege*"). He read it and was converted.[18]

Mario Praz has singled out this final imagery as the best of Crashaw's Baroque imagery found anywhere in his poetry. In these last lines, the poet's "yearning for ecstasy is so powerful and desperate that he almost seems to have reached it."[19] In the course of seventeenth century literature, writes Praz, "there is no higher expression of that spiritualization of sense which is condensed here in a portentous, dizzy soaring of red-hot images" (Praz 262). The poem ends in a mystical explosion which Praz describes as typically Baroque: "The Baroque tries, by multiplication of sensory impressions, to exhaust the sensory and to suggest the presence of the spiritual" (Praz 131).

The Baroque status of the poem does not depend only on this last imagery but characterizes the entire poem. However, the possibility of conversion, or of an ecstatic- erotic religious experience, based on an act of reading seems questionable. Unlike Augustinian conversion, which is based on applying a reading of Scripture to one's life, Crashaw's conversion is based on reading "correctly" the events of Saint Teresa's martyrdom. As I have pointed out, the poet was critical of the interpretation of the painter and advised his readers to read the figure of Teresa in the place of the Seraph. He believes that to the seraph should be given the feminine attributes of Teresa, and she should get the manly ones of the seraph. However, as Alexandra Finn-Atkins observes in her study of Crashaw's "Teresa Trilogy," this is not the case. Evidence shows that the painter got it right and that it is Crashaw who, willingly, misrepresents events to make Teresa a manlier figure and the seraph passive and timid. As Finn-Atkins makes clear, in quoting from Saint Teresa's work, the seraph had the dart with which he wounded her, "I saw, that he had a long Dart of gold in his hand and... thrust it, some several times, through my verie Hart, after such a manner, as that it passed the verie inwards, of my Bowells." (Quoted by Finn-Atkins 20). Crashaw's version of the events of the Saint's Life, which he advises his readers to follow, departs radically from them. His advice to exchange Teresa for the Seraph is his own wish and desire which captures the spirit of the event, as he saw it, rather than the literal facts. His version of the life of Saint Teresa is not an imitation of the facts but only his interpretation. The painter got it "wrong" because he read it literally but not spiritually, or allegorically, as the poet does. Crashaw aimed, instead, at reaching out for the "Flaming heart" of Saint Teresa which can only be represented allegorically. The spiritual can be alluded to but not represented. Praz is correct in stating that that the poet "almost seems to have reached "ecstasy because the act of reading which make it possible makes it allegorically impossible.

If the "Flaming Heart" was a traditional poem, as the other two in the trilogy are, one could read this poem traditionally, or symbolically, as another poem about Teresa of Avila's life. As it is, the poem is a "reading" of her life and all that the poet can do is to teach his readers to read the life of Saint Teresa allegorically, and not literally, as the painter did. Conversion is not made possible just by an act of reading but, as Saint Augustine teaches, allegorically, through Grace, which was probably the case when Crashaw converted. As for the possibility of following Crashaw's instructions to grasp the "true" essence of Saint Teresa's "Flaming Heart," the reader is limited to the inscription of the poem's title. Since language is not symbolic but allegorical, and while one can easily read one figure for another, Saint Teresa for the Seraph, or the Seraph for Saint Teresa, the allegory marks the distance from the event, and the impossibility, to ever be able to recapture it.

Recent Literary Criticism on Metaphysical poetry

My reading of some representative poems by Donne, Marvell and Crashaw, which are known under the category of "metaphysical," but ought to be more properly defined "Baroque," has shown some common traits: their use of unique imagery to surprise and astonish the reader; the theme of love with erotic and metaphysical, if not religious, implications; an excess of intellectual or even scholarly knowledge, and the use of great many devices and conceits. Rosemond Tuve, in *Elizabethan and Metaphysical Imagery,* discusses the influence of Ramist logic on metaphysical imagery and analyzes the functional value of this imagery and concludes that the common characteristics of metaphysical imagery are: "aptness, subtlety, accuracy of aim, disregard of the superficially pleasing, logic power, ingenious or startlingly precise relationships or parallels, a certain 'obscurity' due to logical complexity."[20] When referring to the metaphysical conceit, Mourgues points out that "it is easy to see that it accounts for the intellectual element in metaphysical poetry, its analytical tendency, its difficult subtlety, its use of scholastic modes of reasoning, and its learned imagery" (De Morgues 9). From the functional perspective, these characteristics, carried out by metaphysical conceits, serve to "enter into a solid union and at the same time to maintain their warring identity."[21] In this sense, Mourgue claims, "the term metaphysical becomes a general term, since this kind of poetry is bound up with universal problems of mankind and may therefore be found in any country and at any time" (Mourgue 9). It could also be defined, Baroque.

In the twentieth century there was a shift in attitude toward the English Metaphysical poets by the intervention of T. S. Eliot. In his essay "The Metaphysical Poets," a review of Herbert Grierson's book on *Metaphysical Lyrics and Poems of the Seventeenth Century: Donne to Butler*,[22] T. S. Eliot shed new light on metaphysical poets by claiming that they did not represent a digression from the mainstream of English poetry, but rather a continuation: "the poets of the seventeenth century (up to the Revolution) were the direct and normal development of the precedent age." He claimed that metaphysical poetry is distinguished from other poetry by its unification of sensibility, "which subsequently disappeared, but ought not have disappeared."[23] By "sensibility" Eliot did not mean, merely, feelings, emotions or capabilities of grasping sensual impressions, but that synthetic faculty that can amalgamate and unite thought and feeling, which can fuse remote and even contradictory experiences into a new integration. He also proposed a theory of the "dissociation of sensibility" of eighteenth and nineteenth century English poetry, which is characterized by "the difference between the intellectual poet and the reflective poet" (Eliot 64). His famous quotation, "A thought to Donne was an experience; it modified his sensibility. When a poet's mind is perfectly equipped for its work, it is constantly amalgamating disparate experience" (Eliot 65), implies that the metaphysical poets had a mechanism of sensibility that enabled them to assimilate and fuse the most disparate and heterogeneous experiences into new integrations. They could feel their thoughts and express them through sensuous imagery. In their metaphysical poems, poets like Donne, Marvell and Crashaw, were able to express their thoughts and ideas by embodying them in sensuous, and always erotic, imagery. It is mainly through their use of sensual imagery that the unification of sensibility found its way in characterized expression.

Recent criticism of Metaphysical Poets has certainly progressed from the days of Dr. Johnson. Critics are no longer biased against a group of poets who seemed to stray from traditional Renaissance and Elizabethan poetry. There has been no attempt, however, in contemporary criticism to make amends to Dr. Johnson's derogatory term of "metaphysical" or to approach these poets as (Baroque) poets. What is excluded in many contemporary studies is the poetical. Katrin Ettenhuber in her study of St. Augustine's influence on John Donne – a very scholarly work which analyzes how every work of Augustine can be traced in Donne's poetry, does not say much about Donne's poetry.[24]

Gary Kuchar's study on George Herbert's religious work and the relation of poetry and Scripture in seventeenth century England does not touch on the Baroque potential of this relation.[25] The same goes for Kuchar's other work on the poetry about religious sorrow in early modern England.[26] However, both works are outside the object of my study. The work of Louis L. Martz comes closer to address the issue of Baroque but his study, *From Renaissance to Baroque: Essays on Literature and Art*, touches on the relation of literature and art, but is mainly concerned with the plastic arts rather than literature or poetry.[27] Martz understands the Baroque as an artistic and not as a poetic phenomenon.

The only critic that comes closer to the topic is Hugh Grady's *John Donne and Baroque Allegory: The Aesthetics of Fragmentation.*[28] This is a very important study which discusses one of the major exponents of Baroque literature, Walter Benjamin, and his seminal work on the *Origins of German Baroque Drama.*[29] Grady sees a connection between Benjamin and Donne, by way of Baudelaire, who has been compared to Donne. Grady likes to claim that Benjamin's theory "can help illuminate the poetry of John Donne and contribute to developing new directions in John Donne's studies" (Grady 2). What appears to interest Grady, however, is not so much Benjamin's theory of allegory as the way he was able to combine formalism with cultural, social and political studies (Grady 3). He quotes Benjamin that the function of artistic form is "to make historical content…into a philosophical truth," and he concludes that Benjamin's work is "fundamentally formalist and historicist" as well as "presentist."(Grady 4) According to this "presentist" view, our knowledge of the past changes as our culture changes and develops. This implies, for Grady, that our knowledge of John Donne will vary accordingly to what are the dominant views of the twenty-first century. Or, "it is better to say," adds Grady, what twenty-first century Donne we will ourselves construct" (Grady 4).

What Grady "constructs" is a historicist Benjamin who is a far cry from the allegorical Benjamin on the German *trauerspiel.* The notion of "fragmentation" that he derives from Benjamin and applies to Donne bears no comparison to the fragmentation which characterizes the allegorical character of the German *trauerspiel.* In Benjamin, the notion of fragment derives from his concept of allegory, which is not only ahistorical but also points to the impossibility of history: a history which is death and decay. This is not at all what we have in John Donne. In my view, as I have indicated, Benjamin's type of allegory is closer to the late poetry of Meng Jiao.

In discussing the differences and similarities between Metaphysical and Baroque poetry, Grady dismisses the Baroque in favor of using the term "metaphysical." He believes that the differences are only a question of terminology and not of poetic styles. Even though the Baroque is the more internationally accepted term, both in literature and in the arts, the term "metaphysical" is an "arbitrary term," and not a clear concept, "[the Baroque] became, as its usage proliferated, more a cluster of associations and judgments than a clear concept of its own" (Grady 17). In trying to historicize the term, Grady finds that there is very little consensus today on what the term means. He quotes Gregg Lambert's study on the Baroque to the effect that the term is not historical but has no other mode of existence than literary expression and that the Baroque is essentially an "empty category," which has played havoc "with the empirical assumptions as the basis of historical narration" (Lambert quoted by Grady 17).

In conclusion, this survey of contemporary critical appraisals of "metaphysical poets" may gain from taking a look at Gregg Lambert's work on the Baroque and at the reasons for his dismissal of the Baroque.[30] Lambert rightly relates the Baroque to modernity but he believes that we are at the end of our modernity and already in the postmodern era. Thus, according to him, both modernity and the Baroque are no longer viable forms, namely, "that a certain tradition of modernist experimentation is no longer possible" (Lambert, 146). He concludes his study on the return of the Baroque in modern culture, by stating that the return of the Baroque may very well be "the last sign of our own fading modernity, which, in or at the end, can also be compared to a flawed and imperfect pearl" (Lambert 149).

We observe in Lambert what we have said earlier of the other critics of the Baroque, namely, that the main problem is in historicizing the term. Even when one understands that we are dealing with a poetic style, even when in Lambert the Baroque is conceived as a modernist concept, when we understand the term historically we are still dealing with a style whose time has come. In all these cases, what is being avoided is the poetic or allegory, or, which is the same, the Baroque.

Notes

[1] Herbert Grierson, J. C. *Metaphysical Lyrics and Poems of the Seventeenth Century: Donne to Butler,* (Oxford: Oxford University Press, 1928), xv-xvi.
[2] Odette De Mourgues. *Metaphysical Baroque and Precieux Poetry,* (Oxford: Oxford University Press, 1953), 9.
[3] The first edition of John Donne's collected poems, printed in 1633, two years after he died, were later called *Songs and Sonnets.* It showcases Donne's dazzling range of poetic themes and styles, from works of religious devotion to intellectual wit, cynicism and sexual passion. There are 12 of his Holy Sonnets, as well as Elegies, Satires and a number of famous verses such as "The Flea," "The Good Morrow" and "The Sun Rising". All the texts of John Donne's poems quoted in this chapter are from *The Complete Poetry of John Donne.*
[4] Theodore Redpath. *The Songs and Sonnets of John Donne,* (London: Methuen. 1983), 175.
[5] See Helen Gardner. *The Elegies and The Songs and Sonnets,* (Englewood Cliffs, NJ: Prentice-Hall, 1962).
[6] Harold Bloom. *John Donne: Comprehensive Research and Study Guide,* (Broomall: Chelsea House Publisher, 1999), 16.
[7] See chapter three for a discussion of the Baroque concept of "maraviglia."
[8] Jack Dalglish. *Eight Metaphysical Poets,* (London: Heinemann, 1963), 171.
[9] Nigel Smith. *The Poems of Andrew Marvell,* (Harlow: Pearson Education, 2007), xvii.
[10] Smith, *The Poems of Andrew Marvell,* 75.
[11] Derek Hirst and Steven Zwicker. "Imagining Andrew Marvell," 371-395.
[12] Husain Itrat. *The Mystical Element in the Metaphysical Poets of the Seventeenth Century,* 180.
[13] According to the 1652 version, the poem has the subtitle: "Persuading her to Resolution in Religion, and to render herself without further delay in the Communication of the Catholic Church". According to the *Norton Critical Edition of Seventeenth Century British Poetry: 1603-1660,* there are two versions of the poem and both versions are parodies of the seduction poem. Here I follow the *Norton Critical Edition* version.
[14] George Walton Williams. *The Complete Poetry of Richard Crashaw,* (New York: New York University Press, 1972), 146-153.
[15] G. W. Williams. Ibid.
[16] Saint Teresa of Avila (1515-82). *The Life of Saint Teresa of Jesus,* Trans. David Lewis. (London: T. Baker, 1904), 427-428.
[17] On the Teresa trilogy see Alexandra Finn-Atkins, *The Redemptive Act of Reading: Richard Crashaw and the Teresean Liturgy.* The three poems of the

trilogy are "The Hymne, "An Apologie for the fore-going Hymne" and "The Flaming Heart."

[18] See Saint Augustine, *Confessions*, Book VIII. St. Augustine was widely read in Britain and had a great impact on the religious beliefs of metaphysical poets, especially John Donne. See Katrin Ettenhuber. *Donne's Augustine: Renaissance cultures of interpretation.* (Oxford: Oxford University Press. 2011).

[19] Mario Praz. *The Flaming Heart,* (New York: Norton, 1973), 261-62.

[20] Rosemond Tuve. *Elizabethan and Metaphysical Imagery,* (Chicago: University of Chicago Press, 1961), 353.

[21] Tuve quotes from J.C. Smith who explains that each of the most famous metaphysical conceits by John Donne and Marvell can be reduced to a metaphysical problem. See J.C. Smith, "On Metaphysical Poetry," *Scrutiny*, Dec. 1933.

[22] Grierson and Fowler. *Metaphysical Lyrics and Poems of the Seventeenth Century.*

[23] T. S. Eliot. "The Metaphysical Poets" in *Selected Prose of T. S. Eliot,* (New York: Harcourt Brace Jovanovich, 1975), 63.

[24] Katrin Ettenhuber. *Donne's Augustine: Renaissance Cultures of Interpretation,* (Oxford: Oxford University Press. 2011).

[25] Gary Kuchar. *George Herbert and the Mystery of the Word: Poetry and Scripture in Seventeenth-century England.* (Cham: Palgrave Macmillan. 2017).

[26] Gary Kuchar. *The poetry of Religious Sorrow in Early Modern England.* (Cambridge: Cambridge University Press. 2008).

[27] Louis L. Martz. *From Renaissance to Baroque: Essays on Literature and Art.* (Columbia: University of Missouri Press. 1991).

[28] Hugh Grady. *John Donne and Baroque Allegory: the Aesthetics of Fragmentation.* (Cambridge: Cambridge University Press, 2017).

[29] Walter Benjamin. *The Origin of German Tragic Drama,* (London: Verso. 2009).

[30] Gregg Lambert. *Return of the Baroque in Modern Culture.* (London: Continuum, 2004).

Chapter 2

Mid-Late Tang Baroque Poetry

In his introduction to the translation of Meng Jiao's poems, David Hinton writes that the poet: "opened an imaginative space so original it began an alternative tradition, a tradition which included a number of major poets, and at least two great ones: Li He and Li Shangyin."[1] This alternative tradition of employing quasi-surreal and symbolist techniques to explore ways of being and their relation to the universe ended with the death of Li Shangyin in 858, although his influence continued well into the next Song dynasty. Meng Jiao's poems combine symbolist poetics, linguistic density and ambiguity with intense surreal imagery, which give his poems a quality of expression that conventional language fails to articulate. These qualities make Meng Jiao the first of three major poets of the Mid-Late Tang Dynasty to be discussed in this chapter.

Li He, the second poet, was a younger contemporary of Meng Jiao, and one of the most imitated mid-Tang poets for his grotesque style of poetry which is filled with fantastic and unusual imagery, full of inauspicious words as "old" and "death." He wrote numerous poems about love but also about ghosts and the supernatural world, none of which are in regulated verse. His poems, described by Fusheng Wu as the "poetry of Beautiful women and ghastly ghosts," adopt and transform the eroticism of the Palace Style poetry of the Southern Dynasties, but are also characterized by the peculiar theme and imagery of love of death.[2] The sensuality, eroticism and the treatment of poetry as a sophisticated craft, together with the macabre imagery and diction that make his poems ambiguous and obscure, make of Li He the other major poet of the Mid-Tang Dynasty.

The third poet I discuss is Li Shangyin, a Late Tang poet whose death puts an end to the tradition Meng Jiao started and Li He pursued. Li Shangyin is probably the most complex and ambiguous Chinese poet. His use of Buddhism lore, historical and literary scholarship, obscure but luxurious images, intellectual and witty diction, make his poems beautiful but also extremely ambiguous and difficult to interpret. These three poets exemplify not only the best of Mid-Late Tang Poetry but also what I call Baroque poetry and Baroque poetics.

Meng Jiao: Benjaminian Allegory

Meng Jiao (751-814) is usually regarded a minor poet and is always excluded from the polished and gracious tradition of Chinese literary history. He was born in southern China at the time of the disorders caused by military defeats on borders (751), and later by the An Lushan Rebellion (755-763), which brought about the decline and the eventual demise of the Tang dynasty. Meng Jiao spent the first half of his life as a recluse till he moved his family to Luoyang, the Eastern capital of the dynasty and the center of culture and the arts. He was around forty years old when he moved at the request of his mother, who wanted him to get a respectful government position through the *Jinshi* 進士exam, the national exam for recruitment in the government. It was in Luoyang that he met Han Yu (768-824), the famous essayist, poet and critic, who advocated the emulation of the antique style of lyric poetry.

Although Meng was highly regarded as a major poet in Han Yu's poetic circle and received frequent financial support and job recommendations, his life was spent in misfortune and adversity. He did not pass the exam until his third attempt in 796, when he was forty-five years old; and not until four years later he was assigned a low rank paid position far away from his family, which he did not hold for long. He had children late in life but all three of them died young, and eventually also his wife died. He was unemployed after he resigned from his post and remained poor all his life. His poetry is full of cold and dark feelings, grotesque imagery and contrived expressions with a despair that comes from anger and disappointment. The poems he wrote in his later years, when he lived in Luoyang, employ surrealist and symbolist techniques that bring to his poetry a deep sense of introspection on life and death. David Hinton, in the introduction to his translation collection of Meng's late poems remarks that: "This desperate situation is everywhere in Meng Jiao's work. It appears in Meng's literal descriptions of his world, but more importantly, it is often internalized and transformed into an atmosphere of loss and disorientation" (Hinton xii).

About five hundred of his poems have survived, most of them are lyric verses according to the old *Yuefu*樂府 style. Meng Jiao, however, was very fond of grouping poems together into a narrative. He has many of these group poems, some as many as fifteen poems under one title. The narrative sequence is not itself straightforward or logical. It's allegorical. I have quoted only one poem from each narrative series but I have also tried to give a sense of the whole. The three poems I have chosen are "Cold Creek" (III) 寒溪九首之三, "Autumn Thoughts" (VI) 秋懷十五首之六 and "Laments of the Gorges" (III) 峽哀十首之三.

Cold Creek

寒溪九首之三 Cold Creek (III)

曉飲一杯酒 After a cup of wine at dawn
踏雪過清溪 I crossed the clear creek stepping snow
波瀾凍為刀 The waves that were frozen into blades
剸割凫與鷖 Cut and killed wild ducks and gulls
宿羽皆翦棄 Feathers sheared and abandoned from the past wings
血聲沉沙泥 Blood and caws sank into sands and muds
獨立欲何語 Standing alone: what did I want to say
默念心酸嘶 My mourning heart cried bitterly
凍血莫作春 The frozen blood shall not fertilize the Spring
作春生不齊 If it does, unequally grow the livings
凍血莫作花 Frozen blood shall not be seen as blooms
作花發孀啼 If it is, the widowed mourn and shed tears
幽幽棘針村 Deep in thorns and brambles, lives the village
凍死難耕犁 Where, frozen to death, is hardly plowed.

(Translated by Pengfei Wang)

Not many English translations of the poem can be easily found, among which two translations come to my attention. One is from Stephen Owen who translated this poem decades ago in his dissertation which later was adapted into his book *The Poetry of Meng Jiao and Han Yu*. The other one is from David Hinton and can be found in his *The Late Poems of Meng Jiao*, a translated selections of Meng Jiao's poems. Both translations are fairly close to the original. Owen translates literally what is there but does not go further. His translation remains somewhat vague and the reader has to imagine the rest of what he reads. Hinton's translation fills in the gaps and makes the poem more readable and more understandable, if not more enjoyable. In his translation, we understand how the waves froze into knives and cut the feathers of ducks and geese. Hinton gives us a narrative, Owen stops short from putting the poem together.

"Cold Creek" is a narrative of nine poems which depict an extremely cold and horrifying landscape, in transition between winter and spring, the first month of the lunar calendar year. The series of poems focus on three major themes: 1) they blame and condemn heaven for the severe cold weather that kills birds and fish and makes people's life harder and more difficult; 2) an admonition and an attempt at dissuading people from collecting the frozen birds and fish for food, as these creatures are killed by heaven and are not suitable to eat as food; 3) a sincere elegy for these dead creatures after he buries them. These poems are not meant to portray Meng Jiao as a naturalist or an animal protectionist. The birds and the fish are symbols of the poet's despair at the reality of his times and his condemnation of its practices. The macabre coldness and death of the fish and the birds are his way of denouncing the disastrous age he lives in and the poor people like him who are made to suffer.

This third poem narrates, specifically, the morning scene when the poet sees the dead birds on the river which froze overnight and their frozen blood in the mud, and the poet's lament at what he saw. The first six lines describe the morning landscape: the poet drinks a cup of wine to keep himself warm from the cold and steps on the snow to cross the creek. When he arrives, he sees the unexpected scene of the frozen river, which is completely different from the one he remembered and he depicted in the second poem. Instead of the beautiful picture he had in mind, the frozen creek is horrifying: feathers of dead birds and blood frozen in the mud. Waves frozen in knife blades, birds killed and their feathers cut off and abandoned. The poet stands alone and does not know what to say. As described in the poem: "Standing along … my mourning heart cried bitterly." The poet's own speech is frozen, as he is overwhelmed by sadness and pain.

The next four lines are somewhat obscure. In *The Poetry of Meng Jiao and Han Yu*, Owen explains: "The unnatural cold spell in early spring has, in spilling the blood of the birds over the landscape, created an unnatural kind of spring rain. Meng Jiao fears that this rain of blood will take the place of normal spring rain, causing the plants to grow unnaturally"[3] Flowers, writes Owen, "associated with sexuality, will give rise to unnatural marriages, to widowhood, which refers back to the 'widow's cry' in the preceding poem, and here may also suggest birds" (Owen, *Meng Jiao and Han Yu,* 144). The unnatural event of the frozen creek, with the death and devastation brought about by the overnight freeze, has created an unnatural spring that will have drastic consequences. Instead of the usual happy spring marriages it will bring an unnatural one and only widowhood. Here Hinton's translation is more helpful. In this desolate land, with its frozen fields, nothing can grow. Usually, winter prepares for spring but this unnatural winter cannot bring about a spring of life and renewal but only one of mourning and death.

The imagery in this third poem is of a decayed, withered, and abandoned landscape. The frozen waves, the abandoned feathers, the frozen blood, the ghostly village of thorns and brambles, communicate the sense of a world dark, bitter and in decay. Poem III is exemplary of the Baroque poetics that characterizes not only the narrative of "Cold creek" but also the poetry of Meng Jiao as a whole.

Autumn Thoughts

秋懷十五首之六 **Autumn Thoughts (VI)**

老骨懼秋月 Old bones are afraid of autumn moon
秋月刀劍棱 The autumn moon has sharpness of blades and swords
纖威不可干 Although thin, the might is not challengeable
冷魂坐自凝 A cold soul gets itself congealed sitting
羈雌巢空鏡 The restrained female has nested in the hollow mirror
仙飆蕩浮冰 A gust of fairy wind sweeps off floating ices
驚步恐自翻 Worrying about falling over terrified steps
病大不敢凌 The heavily-ill dares not get up
單床寤皎皎 Waking up in a single bed by the brightness
瘦臥心兢兢 The skinny lies with a cautious heart
洗河不見水 That is the washing river whose water cannot be seen
透濁為清澄 Through the feculence, is the clarity
詩壯昔空說 Empty words the poems were when they were strong
詩衰今何憑 What to rely on when they are weak now

(Translated by Pengfei Wang)

Similar to the last poem, not many English translations are available for this poem as well. Besides the author's translation offered here, the other two translations I would suggest are from Stephen Owen and David Hinton as well. Both can be found in their books mentioned earlier.

"Autumn Thoughts" is an allegorical narrative of fifteen poems with a single dominant theme: the hard life of the aged who live in poverty and disease. In these poems, the poet depicts the changes in the autumn scenery with bitterness and sadness. The most frequently used words are: old, lonely, bone, ill, autumn, cold and death. He writes of his weakness, coldness, and illness that his aged bones feel, and his hostility for the autumn season. This is also the distress, the helplessness and the loneliness that his aged soul feels, and the hostility for his destiny. The autumn in these poems does not symbolize a bountiful harvest but death and decay. The emotions the poem delivers are terrifying and full of depression and self-pity. In Owen's view, this sixth poem is "mostly fantasy, and as such it is the most difficult of the sequence" (Owen, *Meng Jiao and Han Yu*, 170).

The poem begins with a statement that the poet, the old bone, fears the autumn moon because it has blades of knives and swords. The poet suffers insomnia during the autumn nights that are too cold for him. Why should he fear the autumn moon? Is not the moon usually a beautiful thing to watch? The moon is usually a symbol of beauty during autumn nights, but for the poet, a sleepless and sick old man who worries about his life, the moon becomes a frightening symbol of time holding deadly blades. When the cold moonlit shines on his body, the poet feels that it freezes his soul. He fears time symbolized by the moon at night and the momentum of the moonlight which is like blades of knives and swords. The coldness brought about by the autumn moon has also frozen his soul. Owen places emphasis on the moon more than on the poet himself: "The light is spiritually cold rather than physically cold, hence the rational voice in Meng says the freezing is 'for no reason.' The 'thinness,' *hsien*, of the blade of moonlight is primarily the thinness of a thread – a 'strand of light' will cut the 'single thread of life'" (Owen, *Meng Jiao and Han Yu*, 170). Hinton's reading, instead, places emphasis on the poet who is "helpless against" the unchallengeable moonlight.

The next two lines which depict the moon are ambiguous. Grammatically, the line means: either "a restrained hen-bird builds a nest *under* the moon," or "a restrained hen-bird builds a nest *for* the moon." Owen believes the former and Hinton the latter. Besides the literal meaning, the "restrained female" and "the moon" always remind one of the moon goddess, Chang E, who steals the immortal elixir and levitates to the moon where she has to live alone in the cold.

The next four lines record the poet's reaction to the moonlight in his room. He reveals that he has been seriously ill and worried about his health. He is startled by the moonlight on the floor and afraid that it may blur his sight and he may fall, so he dares not step on it. Owen and Hinton translate these two lines very differently and, to a certain extent, different from the original. Owen gives a subject to the verb 恐*kong* – "I" fear; but he gives the verbal phrase "自翻*zi fan*" a different subject – footsteps: my startle footsteps will fly away of themselves. Hinton actually makes the subject of the "*zi fan*" the footsteps as well, but translates "*zi fan*" together with "驚*jing*" as "startle away." The most controversial translation is the next line: the word "凌*ling*" usually means "(standing) above" or "(stepping) on." Owen translates it as "rise" which is right, although "to the others" seems a little confusing; Hinton translates the line as "can't brave ice" – since the character "*ling*" has the meaning of "ice" when it is used as a noun, but in the line it is a verb. The next line tells of the white moonlight cast on his single bed when he wakes up, and his heart is cautious and frightened. Owen explains "this complicated metaphor" as a contrast between mortal reality and immortal ideality.

The next four lines deliver the main point of the poem, if not of the whole narrative series: the redemptive function of his poetry. The ray of moonlight which seems to frighten the poet is, after all, one and the same with the "washing river whose water cannot be seen." When the moonlight strikes the river, the water almost disappears, and by passing through the dirt, it makes it clear and pure. This is, of course, an illusion. It is the illusion cast by the moonlight that makes the foulness of the river seem clean and pure. The moonlight is another metaphor for Meng's poetry. This is what his poetry appears to do by shedding light on the foulness making it clean. The poet, however, as we have seen, denounces the poetic illusion as frightening, as something that would make him fall. The allegory denounces the illusion of the ray of moonlight that appears to cleanse the foulness to make it pure again, but cannot.

The last two lines denounce this type of "vigorous" symbolic poetry, which the poet employed in the past, but which, in Owen's understanding, was only "empty discourse," or "strong" but only "empty talk," in Hinton's reading. When Meng moved away from the traditional, symbolic poetry of Han Yu and his circle, his poetry, according to Owen, "declined," or became "frail," according to Hinton. His poetry had no longer the support of tradition, as it no longer emulates the ancients, and, by definition, was no longer lyrical. It became allegorical, or, in our reading, Baroque, which is the same. As such, it stands by itself and has nothing to rely on. Then the poet asks: "what to rely on" – is he looking for an answer, or expecting an answer to his final question? Maybe not. This sixth poem is an allegory of the impossibility of poetry to whitewash reality. Poetry, like the moonlight, can provide an illusion of purity, but it also denounces it as an illusion.

Laments of the Gorges

峽哀十首之三 Laments of the Gorges (III)

三峽一線天 Sky in the Three Gorges is a thread line
三峽萬繩泉 Cascades in the Three Gorges are ten thousands thread lines
上仄碎日月 Upwards, it mashes the sun and moon
下掣狂漪漣 Downwards, it crushes waves and billows
破魂一兩點 One or two worn souls scatter

凝幽數百年 For hundreds of years they have been kept still and dim
峽暉不停午 In the Gorges, daylight does not stay even noon
峽險多飢涎 In the Gorges, danger comes with hungry sputa
樹根鎖枯棺 The withered coffins are locked in tree roots
孤骨裊裊懸 With lonely skeletons suspending outside of them
樹枝哭霜棲 The tree branches cry for frost's residence
哀韻杳杳鮮 The sad tunes are always remotely fresh
逐客零落腸 The sporadic feelings of the exiles
到此湯火煎 Are like boiled in stews seeing these
性命如紡績 Life is the thread on the spin
道路隨索緣 Its journey follows the isolated fates
奠淚吊波靈 Sacrificing tears to mourn the Wave Spirit
波靈將閃然 Glitters the Wave Spirit will respond

(Translated by Pengfei Wang)

The narrative of "Laments of the Gorges" is probably the most Baroque group of poems of the Mid-Late Tang. As Frodsham comments, the death imagery in the poem is "typical of the Baroque: its application to the landscape, the giver of life itself, is disconcerting and unpleasant"; "Nature has been stripped off her veil: the universe itself has lost its awesome magic and has become a source of cold conceits. In typical Baroque fashion, the spiritual and the material have become dissociated."[4] Tak-wai Wong does not fully agree with Frodsham. He believes that the poem does not merely depict the natural landscape and that it talks "like the other poems under the same title, about the sorrow in or of the gorges. It expresses an exile's feeling of despair – in terms of the rugged landscape, and of the unusual natural phenomena."[5] He does agree, however, that the poem is Baroque, but he believes that what distinguishes it as a Baroque poem are "the complex imagery structure, the distorted version of 'things', and the tragic fusion of emotion with landscape" (Wong 28). However, both critics are essentially in agreement as they consider "Laments of the Gorges," as well as the others in the series, an excellent example of Tang Baroque poetry.

The poem opens on a scenery that depicts the Three Gorges. The poet's perspective moves from the general to the specific, from a broad view to a narrow focus. The poet first gives a general description of the Three Gorges and, then, he goes in more detail. For Tak-wai Wong, the initial general view provides the poet's true impressions, but he believes that the landscape is probably imaginary, and that the imagery, "uniquely expresses the power of death in conceits of roots and branches" (Wong 27). Of course, everything is imaginary, even the Gorges. It's an allegorical landscape of death and decay.

The poem describes the desolate, arid and death-like landscape of the Three Gorges and their laments through their "ten thousand thread lines" of cascades, which the poet hears, as he passes through them. The Three Gorges are the recipients of memories of the people and the events that took place there, "kept still and dim" over a hundred years in the dark. They are "withered coffins" locked in tree roots, where the branches are "skeletons" that "suspending outside" of the coffins, as "the tree branches cry for frost's residence," adding to the "sad tunes [that] are always remotely fresh."

The latter part of the poem shifts its attention to the poet. Comparing to Wong, David Hinton gives a more interpretive and less literal reading to the latter part of the poem. In Hinton's reading, it becomes clear that the Gorges are now addressing the poet as an "exile" who has finally found his home in these places: "Exile ... you'll simmer in seething flame here." (Hinton, 32) The Gorges are the end of the line for him. His life, "is the thread on the spin," after a journey following "isolated fates," has finally reached its resting place in the Three Gorges. The poem ends with an invitation to the poet to offer his tears as a sacrifice to the water ghosts of the past, and with his invitation to them to accept his tears, by "glitters."

The selected poems I have discussed exemplify the main themes of the allegorical narratives of which they are a part. In all of them, the landscape is dramatically associated with time and death, as they are both destructive. The natural scenery is always twisted and pained with colors of cold, darkness and bitterness, through which the poet communicates his feelings of helplessness and despair. Although Meng does not use many scholastic references, he creates unique expressions and images with simple characters through uncommon combinations, word order, and by coining words and combining them together, obsessively. His poetry expresses mainly the poet's sorrow and idiosyncrasies – he does not mind to portray himself in his startling, ghostly, and elegiac poems as a desperate, creepy old man, ill, and full of self-doubt. Meng Jiao is the quintessential Tang Baroque poet.

Li He: Irony and the Lyric

Li He died at the age of 26 but earned the fame of possessing a "demonic talent" because of his dense and allusive use of symbolism, his sensual and often grotesque imagery, and his unconventional style of poetry. After his death, the two greatest poets of the Late Tang, Du Mu and Li Shangyin, lavished great praise on him and his poetry. Their celebration of Li He created an image of him as a poet completely absorbed by his poetry but indifferent to the social and political implications that made poetry an important asset of mainstream Chinese life during the Tang dynasty. As Owen remarks, "Indeed, he is more a poet when simply left to write poetry. If he works at poetry, it is not the social poetry that is the norm" (Owen, *End of Chinese Middle Ages*, 162).

Li He was born to a remote branch of the imperial house of Tang, which did bring some privileges other than respect. He was talented but he never conformed to the social and literary standards of his day. His official biography in *New History of Tang*新唐書tells how he could write poems at the age of seven and that he was enthusiastically accepted by his contemporaries as a poet. "He never wrote poems on a given topic, forcing his verses to conform to the theme, as others do."[6] He was a talented relative of the imperial house, but he was never accepted to enter the national government exam because of his father's name, *Jinsu*, whose pronunciation sounded like the name of the exam, *Jinshi*, and so the exam became taboo for him. This absurd situation, which evoked great sympathy among his contemporaries, gave him strength for his writing and also determined his lifestyle: a disregard for traditional poetic forms, macabre as well as sensual imagery, his obsession with the eroticism of the Southern Dynasties Palace Style poetry (gongtishi宮體詩), which, most likely, was the cause of his death by "sexual dissipation," according to Frodsham.[7]

The three poems of Li He that I discuss are "Song of Heyang" 河陽歌, one of the most famous yet obscure of his fantasy poems; "Su Xiaoxiao's Tomb"蘇小小墓, a famous ghost poem, with a mixture of eroticism and the macabre; and "Song: A Lovely Woman Combing Her Hair" 美人梳頭歌, an imitation of the Palace Style poetry, full of sensuality and erotic allusions.

Song of Heyang

The poem is obscure and enigmatic. It depicts the scene of a night feast where the poet meets someone he desires. The poem was influenced by other longer regulated verse poems, of the same title, written by Li Shangyin when he was young. Scholars are divided as to what happens in the poem. There are those who believe that the poem recounts events that happened to the poet himself, and those who believe that it is an account of someone else's romance. The title, 河陽歌, "Song of Heyang," refers to Heyang, a location north of the Yellow River. In traditional Chinese poetry, poems named after places, or which contain place-names in their titles, usually invoke some shared lore about the place. But Li He's Heyang does not do that, no lore is related to it, or the lore is lost before it could be annotated.

河陽歌　　Song of Heyang

染羅衣　To dye light silk clothes
秋藍難著色 Autumn Blue is a difficult coloring
不是無心人 Not being a heart-less
爲作臺邛客 but to be a guest of Tai-qiong
花燒中潬城 Flowers in Zhongdan City is blooming flamingly
顏郎身已老 Lover Yan has grown old
惜許兩少年 Regretfully allowing the two youngsters
抽心似春草 Hearts crazily sprouted like the spring grasses
今日見銀牌 In the day today, her silver name plaque was seen
今夜鳴玉讌 In the night tonight, her singing at the banquet was heard
牛頭高一尺 Her hair styled a food high in the Ox-head
隔坐應相見 She should have seen as well even with people sitting in between
月從東方來 The East, moon rose from
酒從東方轉 The east, wine was passed from
觥船飫口紅 Her surfeited red lips on the boat shaped cup
蜜炬千枝爛 Glittered with the thousands of beeswax candles

(Translated by Pengfei Wang)

The poem, as the title indicates, is in verse style. To dye silk clothes with autumn blue is a metaphor to indicate that the feelings between the lovers are not built up quickly, but take time and several interactions. The story related here refers to Zhuo Wenjun卓文君 and Sima Xiangru司馬相如, a famous love story of elopement from the Han dynasty. The "中潬城*Zhong Dan Cheng*," in the third line, is probably the only connection with the title, because it is the name of a fort in the middle of the yellow river in Heyang. When the flowers are in full bloom in this fort, the body of "顏郎*Yan-lang*" is said to have grown old. Yan was a Han dynasty low ranked official who unluckily did not fit the promotion standards set by three generations of emperors and when he finally met an emperor who valued his ability, he was too old to take office. There is some controversy as to whom "*Yan-lang*" refers: some scholars believe that this is a gesture of humility, others believe it refers to a guest at the same feast who was older in age.

The poem mentions two youths. We do not know if they are two singing girls, or the poet and the singing girl, or the singing girl with her lover, whose love sprouts as fast as the spring grass. The phrase "惜許*xi xu*" at the beginning of the seventh line is ambiguous: it could mean either "regret allowing" or "treasure and approve" but in each case, they imply two different readings. If it is "regret," then the fast sprouting love affair should not be allowed, but why? Or it may be a memory: the once fast sprouting love is gone now. If it is "treasure and approve," the fast sprouting love between the two youths must have happened in the past and therefore it can be treasured and approved. Together with the previous two lines: flowers in full bloom make the city look like it is burning in flames – it must be spring time; but Yan's body has grown old, it has an air of shame, pity and helplessness: a man with an old body, in spring time, either regrets allowing a long lost love affair to happen, or recalls the once treasured love with a singing girl.

The next two lines identify the woman with the silver plaque as a licensed singing girl, since, in the Tang dynasty, workers in the state-run entertainment industry were required to wear a silver plaque at their belts, on which their names were inscribed. By the silver plaque one knew who was performing, and at night one could see her serving and singing. The ox-head, "牛頭*niu tou,*" is usually understood as a wine container in the shape of an ox-head. The seat second to the next, "隔坐*ge zuo,*" indicates that they are not sitting together, there is someone in between, but they could see each other. The wine that circles from the east describes, most probably, a drinking game played at the feast. The character "觥*gong*" literally refers to an ancient wine container coming with a spoon, which can be used to distribute the wine in drinking cups. The character "飫*yu*" literally means to be satiated with food, or satiety. The last line depicts a surrealistic scene with "glittered with thousands beeswax candles蜜炬千枝爛."

Frodsham and Owen, both of who have ever translated this poem, have different approaches to the original. Owen's approach is more literal, whereas Frodsham's is more liberal and provides a more acceptable reading of the poem. He explains that Autumn Blue means that the color is dark blue and this is why it is a hard color to dye, it takes several times to get the color right. He also relates "autumn" to "old age" and agrees with Ye Congqi葉蔥奇, a modern scholar, that the poem is about the poet who "considers himself too old for a love-affair with a young girl" (Frodsham, *Poems of Li He,* 152). However, whether or not it is about the poet is irrelevant. It is certainly about someone whose time has passed, as Master Yen who is "old by now."

Frodsham explains in a footnote that he followed the interpretation of the famous Japanese Sinologist Suzuki Taro and believes that this poem is "about two singing girls whom Ho had evidently met some years previously while passing through Ho-yang county, Honan" (Frodsham, *Poems of Li He*, 152). Therefore, his translation of the two youths as "those two young girls," is understandable. So the phrase, "love sprouting like spring grass," literally, "drawing hearts like spring grass" means, in this reading, that the poet is sorry for becoming involved with those two young girls: "I'm sorry I let those two young girls pluck my heart like a spring flower." (Frodsham, *Poems of Li He*, 152)

The feeling one gets from the poem is more a sense of loss deriving from the memory of a past love affair when the two meet again at a feast. Years have passed, the man has grown old, yet the girl is still working as a singing girl in a state-run entertaining house. Once they were madly in love with one another, now the man notices her name on the silver plaque and sees her at her performance at night. They do not sit together, but apart from each other, but he believes she must have seen him as well. The moon rises and drinking goes round and round. The drinking cups are "tired" of the guests' lips, while the candles are shining bright lighting up the room. The wine goes around as always, the entertainment is the same, only people age and change.

Su Xiaoxiao's Tomb

蘇小小墓	**Su Xiaoxiao's Tomb**
幽蘭露	Dews on the orchid in dim
如啼眼	Are like the teary eyes
無物結同心	Nothing to knot a true love with
煙花不堪翦	No cut-off can be applied to fireworks
草如茵	Grass is like her cushion
松如蓋	Pine tree is like her parasol
風為裳	Wind makes her skirt
水為珮	Water makes her pendant
油壁車	Her carriage with oiled sides
夕相待	Waits in the dusk
冷翠燭	The cold king-fisher candles
勞光彩	Waste their light and color
西陵下	At the food of the West Mausoleum
風吹雨	Winds blow rains

(Translated by Pengfei Wang)

Su Xiaoxiao was a famous prostitute who lived during the Southern Qi dynasty (479-502). She was a very good singer and died young of an illness. There have been many stories written about her during her lifetime and after. The earliest surviving writings is a Southern Dynasties ghostly song called "Su Xiaoxiao's Song蘇小小歌":

妾乘油壁車	I ride a coach with oiled sides
郎騎青驄馬	He rides a barley green horse.
何處結同心	Where will we tie a true love knot? –
西陵松柏下	Under the cypress and pine, on West Mount.[8]

(Translated by Pengfei Wang)

The "oiled sides" coach became symbolic of Su Xiaoxiao in all the literature about her. People even believe that the coach was buried with her in the tomb. In this Southern Dynasties song, the "true love knot" is knotted with two laces or belts; it is usually a symbol of the love relation and it is a euphemism for sexual behavior in erotic literature. The other conventional symbols used in the song are "West Mount," the "cypress" and the "pine": West Mount is a cemetery, a place for tombs; cypress and pine are trees people usually associated with tombs. The meaning of the song is that true love can only be fulfilled after death, in the tomb. In the Tang dynasty, there was a version of this story that in stormy nights, when people passed by her tomb, they could hear the sound of singing coming from it. It is believed, however, that Li He never visited her tomb, which is located nowadays either in Jiaxing County or by the West Lake in Zhejiang Province. As Owen writes, Li He's poem is probably "a scene of the mind realized in poetry" (Owen, *Late Tang*, 169).

The poem begins with a strong display of rhetorical showmanship: dew on the orchid, tearing eyes, flowers in mist, carpet-like lawn, skirt of wind, pendant of water, timid candle light in the blue color of a kingfisher's feather, and so on. The detailed description exemplifies the sensuality of the poem, which transforms the poet's dark obsession with death into an aesthetic representation. Fusheng Wu once commented on this poem that Li He "adopts some highly evocative diction and then cancels out its effects by setting it in a very different context. Thus no one would expect the above-mentioned conceits to be used to describe a graveyard scene" (Wu 109). Li He's poem was probably inspired by the old song of the Southern Dynasties, but he goes further. The old song says true love can only be found in death, but Li He says that even in death, one waits in vain for one's true love.

Stephen Owen translated this poem more literally and his literal translation indicates the sense of loss in the endless waiting in vain, which makes the flowers in the mist too piteous to be picked. It seems that it is the flowers' pitiful condition, which is at stake but it is actually the situation described in the previous line: "nothing to knot a true love with." (Owen, *Late Tang*, 169) Owen summarizes his understanding of the poem as follows: "The old singer half materializes, scattered in the scene around her tomb, then in the coach of the old song, and finally as a flickering ghost-light, waiting still – until a gust of wind-blown rain puts out the candle and ends the poem" (Owen, *Late Tang*, 169). In Owen's view, all the flowers, dew, grass, pine, etc. that the poet depicts are all materialized images of the ghost of Su Xiaoxiao, who is waiting in vain for her love because "nothing knot a true love with." However, the ghost still has hopes to attract some passerby when the storm ends. This is a sad and romantic interpretation of the poem, but in the old song, the sounds of music and singing could only be heard in the storm not before or after.

Frodsham gives a different translation, which captures very well the pathos of the poem and the lover's drama who cannot bear to cut the "mist-wreathed flowers" over her tomb because it would be like cutting the lifeline that links him to her. Frodsham describes the tomb that the poet has created out of Nature: the grass that serves as cushions, the pines for awning, the wind as her skirt, and water as her girdle. There is also her "oil-silk carriage" where she is waiting at dusk. Finally, at the end of the poem, we come to see her tomb: "the Western Grave-mound, / Wind-blown rain" (Frodsham, *Poems of Li He*, 30). All this section is described much more crassly and vaguely in Owen whose translation of these last lines does not give the notion that we are looking at a tomb: "At the foot of West Mound/Wind blows the rain" (Owen, *Late Tang*, 169).

Song: A Lovely Girl Combing Her Hair

美人梳頭歌　Song: A Lovely Girl Combing Her Hair

西施曉夢綃帳寒 Xi Shi morning dreams in chill chiffon bed curtains
香鬟墮髻半沉檀 Her scented chignon half falls on the sandalwood pillow
轆轤咿啞轉鳴玉 Jingles of pendants after squeaks from the windlass
驚起芙蓉睡新足 Wake up the lotus blossom from a full sleep
雙鸞開鏡秋水光 The double phoenix cover opens, her mirror, an autumn pond

解鬟臨鏡立象床 Untie her hair knots at the mirror, standing by her ivory bed
一編香絲雲撒地 Strands of fragrant silky hair drop on the floor like clouds
玉釵落處無聲膩 Her jade hairpin falls, no sound unpleasant
纖手卻盤老鴉色 Style and knot the old rook color with her slim fingers
翠滑寶釵簪不得 Sleek as jade, her jewelry hairpins cannot hold
春風爛漫惱嬌慵 The pleasant breezes annoy her pampered slapdash
十八鬟多無氣力 Eighteen knots exhaust all her energy
妝成婑鬌欹不斜 Her beautifully styled hair leans just right
雲裾數步踏雁沙 In cloud skirt she counts her steps toward the Geese on Sands
背人不語向何處 Turning her back to others silently, where is she going –
下階自折櫻桃花 Downstairs to pick herself a twig of cherry blossoms.

(Translated by Pengfei Wang)

This is probably one of the best versions of Palace Style poetry in Li He's poetry. Palace Style has often been criticized for objectifying women, especially by Palace Style poets who usually adopted the descriptive techniques of the "Poetry on Things" (*yong wu shi*詠物詩), where women are usually represented as precious toys. The scenes of women putting on make-up are the most common subjects of this type of poetry. One of the most probable sources of Li He's inspiration is Xiao Gang, Emperor Jianwen of Liang (503-551), "A Lovely Woman's Morning Toilette" 美人晨妝詩.[9]

北窗向朝鏡 The north window faces her morning mirror,
錦帳復斜縈 Twisted brocade curtains slant down by her bed.
嬌羞不肯出 Coy and shy she is reluctant to come out,
猶言妝未成 And says her make up is not yet complete.
散黛隨眉廣 Kohl broadens with her eyebrows,
胭脂逐臉生 Red rouge comes to life on her cheeks.
試將持出眾 I bet she will be outstanding in the crowd,
定得可憐名 And surely will win a fame for her adorableness.[10]

(Translated by Pengfei Wang)

Many of the clichés of Palace Style poetry can be found in this short poem: the appreciation of the woman's beauty and her shyness, her person, not because of who she is but because she is observed in detail as an object. As Fusheng Wu writes: "The almost rude intrusion by the poet in the last couplet indicates that the focus of the poem is actually not the woman, as the title suggests, but the poet, because the description of her manners in the first six lines only serves to advance the poet's hypothesis about this woman in the last two lines. It is he, the observer, who has the last word" (Wu 82). However, Li He is not just an imitator, but an innovator of this type of poetry, although he did imitate its conceits. The title of the poem is typical of this erotic style, which takes as its central theme the scene of a beauty combing her hair. Differently from Xiao, Li He's poem is not concerned with the whole make-up, but with only one stage: the combing of her hair in the style she prefers.

I have compared two translations, one by Frodsham, the other by Fusheng Wu. The two translators have different understandings of some of the key terms and their use in the poem. Fusheng Wu's translation is comparatively accurate since it is probably based on Wu's reading of Xiao's poem. By comparison, Frodsham's version is more interpretative and in general a better translation.

The first four lines depict the scene of the woman getting up after a night's sleep. She is as beautiful as Xi Shi西施, but she wakes up with her yesterday's hairstyle out of shape: *duoji*墮髻, a popular Tang woman hairstyle, half- loose. As she gets up, the bed creaks; the jade pendants hanging from the bed curtain ring as well. Now she is fully awake. The next four lines describe her undoing of her half-loose hairstyle but not before she opens her covered mirror on the dresser. The mirror is decorated with a pair of phoenix on its cover and is clear and bright as the autumn water. She loosens her unshaped hairstyle standing in front of her mirror by the ivory bed. When she succeeds in doing so, the end of her long hair falls like clouds cast on the floor, and her jade hairpin slides on the floor without making a noise. She, then, redoes her hairstyle: her long thin fingers are working on her hair, which is as black as a raven's feather. The color of raven's feather is a common and popular image for a woman's hair, but the acceptable phrase should be the color of "a young rook's feather," not an old one, which is used in the poem, which indicates her age. Her hair is so smooth and silky that her hairpins do not hold and stay. She gets impatient because of her indolence and she is too tired to make the eighteen-coil hairstyle with eighteen knots. The concluding lines tell us what she does after her hair is styled and she gets up. She steps out of the room toward the tempos of the music, "the Geese on Sands." The music full title is "Wild Geese Alighting on a Sandy Shore 平沙落雁," which is a very famous ancient song, and one of its authors is said to be the early Tang poet Chen Ziang (659-700). Where is she going? Downstairs: to pick a small branch of cherry blossoms.

From this brief description, we can see that there are essential differences between Li He's poem and its Palace Style's model. Instead of a static description of the woman's manners, the woman in Li He's poem moves dynamically. Zhu Ziqing explains Li He's innovation of Palace Style poetry as adopting the device "of using eccentric and obscure conceits to complement the shortcomings of superficiality and the eroticism of the Palace Style."[11]

In my translation, I accept Frodsham's introduction to the chignon, which was very popular among women in the Tang dynasty. The women's hairstyles in this period became higher and higher, and women used chignon to decorate, shape and make their hair taller because usually their own hair could not meet the standards of high hairstyles. The Late Tang poet Lu Guimeng 陸龜蒙 (?-881) wrote: "All the girls in town wear hair one foot in height, not just mine is high."[12]

Li He modeled his poem on the Palace Style's "Morning Toilette" poetry but his version is not only radically different but it is also an affectionate description of the woman who is no longer in her youth. His portrait of the old courtesan transpires, gradually and indirectly, through indirect details that do not seem to apply to her at first, such as, "her mirror, an *autumn* pond," to indicate that she is no longer young, but in the "autumn" of her years.

Her dreams at dawn are, perhaps, erotic, reminders of her better days and of a love she can no longer expect. Her age shows in that she is late in rising and by her fallen chignon. The color of her rook hair is described as "old." As I have indicated, the color of rook's feather was a common and popular image for a woman's hair, but for a young woman the phrase for hair would be of "young" rook's color, not an old one, as in this case. Her "old rook" matches her beauty which is just as old. Because of her age, her toilet becomes a chore. After trying eighteen knots or more, she has no strength left. Her toilet done, she sits firmly and "does not slip," as she sometimes does. She is careful in stepping out, like a "goose alighting on a sandy shore," at the rhythm of the music of "The Geese on Sands," an ancient piece that she probably danced at when she was young. When she was young, after finishing her toilet, she probably would step out in the crowd to be admired, as the Palace Style poem has it: "I bet she will be outstanding in the crowd,/ And surely will win a fame for her adorableness." That time is long past. The poet brings up the question of where she could be going now that she has finished her toilet: "Where is she going?" The implication is that because she is old, she has nowhere to go. The reply, which reflects the general pathos of the poem, is nowhere too far, just a few steps away to pick herself, "a twig of cherry blossom." This is the only big event for which she has spent all morning doing her hair. This is all that she can expect of her day, now that she is no longer young and beautiful. Li He does not tell us directly that she is old and no longer an object of admiration. He describes her going through the steps of doing her hair revealing her age, indirectly. He takes a traditional Palace Style's "Morning Toilette" poem and reveals, through irony, the woman behind the object.

These three poems are representatives of Li He's poetry and of his poetic technique that I am calling Baroque because they are not mimetic representations of people or events but are allegories of the impossibility of love or true love. In the "Song of Heyang" it is the difficulty, if not the impossibility, to dye silk clothes in the shade of "Autumn Blue," namely, of a love affair with someone younger, or of a different status. The poem "Su Xiaoxiao's Tomb" is about the impossibility of true love by collapsing the image of her "carriage with oiled sides" with her tomb, where she waits for her true love in vain. The third poem, "Song: A Lovely Girl Combing her Hair," is about a lovely girl who turns out to be not so young and who no longer expects anything from life or from love. All that is left for her to do is to go through her everyday routine of doing her hair, as she has always done, but this time only to just go down a few steps in her garden to pick herself a spray of cherry blossom.

Li Shangyin: Allusion as Disruption

Ever since the early Song Dynasty (960-1279), about a century after his death, Li Shangyin was regarded one of the most influential late Tang poets. During his life time (813-858), however, his poetic genius went unrecognized. About six hundreds of his poems from circulating manuscripts have survived, which were not collected and published by Li himself, or by his family after his death. The earliest annotated collection of his poems is an early Qing Dynasty collection, about seven centuries after his death, although several collections, mentioned in different sources, have been lost. His poetry is mainly known for its obscure and ambiguous imagery and meaning, whose main theme is enduring love and the temporality of all things. His poems are usually written in interlinked layers of meaning, with facts interwoven with memories and references to ancient lore, unknown or not readily definable symbols, imagistic language and diction, which may refer to some code now lost, to construct a world of dazzling exteriority and cryptic interiority.

Li Shangyin writes in the declining phase of the great Tang dynasty, in its last attempt to assert authority and control over the local warlords. Although Li served for a short time as a low ranking official in imperial offices, he spent most of his life as one of the intellectuals who served different local warlords, and usually in the rural provinces. His career never brought him a high position and, in his last years, he quit his position because of failing health. He writes on various occasions and topics, and mainly for a small intimate circle of readers. Most of his lyrical poems, known in traditional Chinese poetry, as "無題 *Wu Ti,*"

"Without Title" or "Untitled" are about unrequited love. Their obscure imagery is usually linked to some well-known ancient lore, and the results are short but densely poetical rhymes that evoke strong feelings in the reader.

The poems I have chosen to illustrate the "Baroque" aspects of his poetry are his well-known, "The Ornamented Zither," one of his most widely known and recognized poems, which although has a title, is one of the poems "without title"; the second poem is "Written on a Monastery Wall," apparently, on Buddhism, and not very well-known; the thirds poem is "Lamp," one of his "Poems on Things." Once again I quote the poems in the Chinese original with my own translations for each poem and provide comments on two other potential readings or, at least, two different perspectives.

The Ornamented Zither

The poem is named after the first two characters of the first line, which is a tradition of naming Li Shangyin's poems without titles, not to confuse them with those known as "無題 *Wu Ti*," meaning literally "No Title," "Without Title," "Untitled," or "Missing Title."

錦瑟 The Ornamented Zither

錦瑟無端五十弦 The brocade zither, with no reason, has fifty strings
一弦一柱思華年 Each string and each bridge yearn for flowering years
莊生曉夢迷蝴蝶In his morning dream, Zhuangzi gets confused with a butterfly
望帝春心托杜鵑 With his spring heart, Emperor Wang entrusts to cuckoos
滄海月明珠有淚 Under the bright ocean moon, peals shed tears
藍田日暖玉生煙 In the warm Blue-mountain sun, jade generates smoke
此情可待成追憶This feeling should have possibly become a lingering memory
只是當時已惘然 While at that time, it had already been lost in the bewildered.

(Translated by Pengfei Wang)

James Liu includes this poem and translates it in his study of Li Shangyin as a Baroque poet. Liu's translation of the title, "Ornamented Zither," places emphasis on the ornamental, rhetorical, or allegorical character of the poem. Stephen Owen, the other translator that easily found, plays down the rhetoric of the poem by translating it "The Brocade Zither" (Owen, *Late Tang*, 394).

The original Chinese title contains two characters: 錦瑟 *jin se*. 錦*jin*, literally means "brocade," but when it is used as an adjective, it means luxuriously decorated; 瑟*se*, is an ancient musical instrument with twenty-five strings and movable bridges. The rectangle-shaped instrument when it is being played is usually horizontally placed on a table and occasionally across the knees. The zither is the main symbol of the poem. In the first line, the zither is said to have had fifty strings which is not the case because it is a twenty-one strings instrument in modern time. The reference is to an ancient legend when the zither had fifty strings. The story goes that when the god Tai-di (Emperor Tai) asked the goddess Su-nu (the White Maid) to play it, the tunes were so bitterly sad that they brought great grief to both of them. Tai-di, then, ordered the instrument to be broken into two halves, and since then, the instrument has only twenty-five strings.

Owen's translation of the first line underplays the importance of the mythic origins of the zither stating that "it just happens" (Owen, *Late Tang*, 393) to have had fifty-strings. James J. Y. Liu's translation, "for no reason," (Liu, *Poetry of Li Shangyin*, 51) undermines the origins of the legend by stating that the zither had fifty strings, for no reason. The importance of the zither is stated in the second line which links the strings and bridges to the recollection of youthful years. From the legend it is clear that the recollection of these years is not happy or pleasant. The zither's power of recollection is ironic since, as we know from the legend, its sound was so sad and so devastating that the god decided to split the instrument in half.

The recollection of youthful years is the substance of the poem and the subject of the next two couplets are stories of tragic and unrequited love. The first story narrates the famous allegory of Taoist master Zhuangzi who once dreamed of being a butterfly. When he woke up, he was not sure whether he was Zhuangzi dreaming to be a butterfly or a butterfly dreaming to be Zhuangzi. James J. Y. Liu captures well the confusion of Master Chuang after his dream: "Master Chuang was confused by his morning dream of the butterfly." (Liu, *Poetry of LiShangyin*, 51) Owen, however, states that Zhuang Zhou was "lost in a butterfly." (Owen, *Late Tang*, 394)

The second line tells the story of Emperor Wang of Shu who had a love affair with his prime minister's wife and killed himself out of shame. After his death, his amorous heart, in James Liu's version, was "entrusted to the cuckoo." (Liu, *Poetry of Li Shangyin*, 51) In Owen's translation the "amorous heart" becomes "spring heart," and in a more literal rendering, it is "lodged in a cuckoo." (Owen, *Late Tang*, 394)

The next two stories deal more directly with the theme of unrequited love. In one legend, it is said that in nights of full moon, oysters open and show their pearls to absorb the moonlight to make them shine. When the moon wanes, the pearls lose their gleam and hide. Another legend gives a more human and less literal meaning. It is said that on nights of a full moon, mermaids weep and their tears become pearls in the moonlight. This is James Liu's version. Owen's translation is somewhat vaguer as he translates that there are "tears" in "pearls." (Owen, *Late Tang*, 394)

The next story is one of unrequited love. It tells the story of Purple Jade, the daughter of the King of Wu, who refused to marry her to the man she loved. Jade killed herself and when she reappeared and her mother tried to embrace her she vanished from her arms like smoke. Li Shangyin connects the legend to The Indigo Field, "藍田 *lan tian*," a mountain famous for the fine jade that can be mined there. In poetry, there is a world which resembles the Indigo Field Mountain in warm sunshine. One can only look at the jade from a distance but when one comes too close, it disappears.

The two couplets make up the substance of the youthful years recollected by the poem's zither. Just as in the case of the mythic fifty string zither, the recollection is certainly nothing to be recollected. However, the feeling that was supposed to reach the subject at the end of the poem never does. As we are told, the poet, or whoever is intended in the last line of the poem, was already "lost in the bewildered." Not only the sound of the zither fails to reach the poet, but it would seem that the poet has no need of the fifty-string zither to remind him of his bitter youthful years.

Li Shangyin's the "Ornamented zither" is not an imitation of the fifty-string zither of old but an allegory of the impossibility of coinciding with it. The poem does not bring about the recollection of the youthful years that it promises but states, at the same time, the instability of a subject that is already "lost in the bewildered." Any attempt, therefore, to read the poem symbolically is bound to fail, just as the poem does. As the poet indicates in the first line, there is "no reason" to recollect his youthful years because they are as sad and as tragic as those experienced by the gods. The poem is an allegory of the impossibility of recollecting one's youthful years, since one is already "lost in the bewildered."

Written on a Monastery Wall

Differently from the "Ornamented Zither," which is one of the most well-known poems of Li Shangyin, this poem is not well-known. The poem is easily categorized among Li's Buddhist poems that he wrote when he was working in

Sichuan and Guangxi, and took up the practice of Buddhism and wrote poems about his new faith and about Buddhist monks.[13] However, the poem is only apparently about Buddhism, even though the first and last couplets are a direct reference to it.

題僧壁 Written on a Monastery Wall

捨生求道有前蹤	There were trails that one gave up their life for the Way
乞腦剜身結愿重	For their wishes, they beg to scarify their brains and bodies
大去便應欺粟顆	The Greatness shall go bigger than a millet grain
小來兼可隱針鋒	The Tininess should be able to hide on a needle tip too
蚌胎未滿思新桂	Unfilled oyster wombs, longing for next crescent moon
琥珀初成憶舊松	Newly produced amber, recalls resin from the previous pine
若信貝多真實語	If sutras on palm leaves are believed true
三生同聽一樓鐘	A same temple bell may be heard throughout past present and future

(Translated by Pengfei Wang)

English translations of this poem are very few. James Liu does not even include it in his study of Li Shangyin where he translates 100 of his poems. Those I have been able to find, however, provide sufficient subject matter for discussion. The first is by Arthur Cooper, who translates it with reference to A. C. Graham's translation of the same poem. Cooper does not state directly why he translated the poem but he was probably prompted by a desire to improve on A. C. Graham's. These translations are interestingly different in many key concepts and enlighteningly undermine my understanding of the original poem.

The poem's title, 題僧壁*ti seng bi*, literally means "writing on a Buddhist monk's wall." The first four characters in the first two lines are Buddhist phrases: "gave up their life for the Way" and "to scarify their brains and bodies," though the literal meaning of the phrase is "beg brain cut body." Both stories are derived from the sutras and they indicate that those who are ready to give up their life and enter the monastic life should be ready to also give up their body and their mind. The middle two couplets are vague. Scholars have turned to the sutras in the hope of finding some possible allusion. Essentially they are maxims. The first implies the wisdom of seeing the world in a grain of sand, here in a grain of "millet," the other points to the reverse: what is small can fit into the Mystic Pinpoint.

The third couplet with the reference to pearls echoes the "Ornamented zither." Here the two translations by Cooper and A. C. Graham part ways. Cooper's translation emphasizes the implied meaning of the first line, namely, that the "womb" of the oyster refers to a woman's: "Oysters, their wombs unfilled,/long for the full moon." (Cooper, 95) A. C. Graham's more literal translation erases this latent meaning: "The oyster before its womb fills thinks of the new cassia." (Graham, 161) The same can be said for the next line. Cooper's translation renders better the meaning alluded to: "And amber until made/ sighs for its past pine." (Cooper, 95) A. C. Graham's translation does not render the main point of the imagery: "The amber, when it first sets, remembers a former pine." (Graham, 161) The point, here, is that amber does not set.

In these last lines, there is a shift from a poem apparently about Buddhism to one about unfulfilled love. The reference to the "unfilled" oyster's womb makes this clear. The same conceit is continued in the reference to amber, which is made from pine resin but does not become amber until it is set, that is, "impregnated" by an insect. The hidden image is another reference to unfulfilled love. The woman waits, like amber, to be impregnated, but the wait is hopeless. Comparatively, Cooper's translation renders very well the longing of the amber, or of the woman, whereas for A. C. Graham this has already happened because he does not see the connection of the amber with a woman's desire. That might be why Cooper felt that he had to re-translate Graham.

The couplet marks a shift from being a poem about leaving life and entering a Buddhist monastery to those women who either by choice or because they wanted to became nuns fill unfulfilled behind the walls of a Buddhist monastery. This shift is clear in Cooper but not in A. C. Graham, who believes he is just translating a Buddhist poem. This is clear in the last stanza, where the issue is faith. In Cooper's translation, if we believe in the Holy Writ of Buddhism, we will hear eternity in the sound of the gong: "But faith in Holy Writ for the true message/ Hears Present, Future, Past/ all in one gong stroke!" (Cooper, 96) A. C. Graham's translation is more literal and more confusing: "If we trust the true and sure words written on Indian leaves/ We hear all past and future in one stroke of the temple bell." (Graham, 161) There is no gong stroke here, which gives a sense of eternity, only a temple bell. But the main point of this last stanza is "faith." If we believe in Buddha and in the eternity that Buddhist faith promises, we will hear the past, the present and the future in a gong stroke. If we are not believers, we won't. It is impossible to say whether Li Shangyin had sufficient faith to hear the Past, the Present and the Future in a gong stroke, but it is certain that those Buddhist women he knew and who were pining away in Buddhist monasteries did not hear it. They only heard, like the amber, the call of the flesh, of their unfulfilled wombs, at the full moon.[14]

Cooper's translation not only lends itself to a better understanding of the poem but it places in evidence the Baroque conceits of the oyster-womb-woman, as well as the amber-pine-insect conceit. What is more, Cooper's translation highlights the irony of the poem in the first lines of the poem, which requires one to "hollow the body" when this is, precisely, what is impossible for these Buddhist nuns. Most important is the title of the poem which is written on a monastery wall. The poem is not meant to be a manifesto to promote Buddhism; on the contrary, it denounces its practice even if only for those Buddhist nuns living within its walls.

Lamp

The "Lamp" is one of Li Shangyin's "Poems on Things." This apparently simple poem is actually quite complex in its implication, which is not readily apparent at first and makes it one of the less translated poems of Li Shangyin. The title of the poem is simple enough: 燈*deng*, Lamp. It is not "a lamp" or "lamps," or "some lamp," but a generic name for all lamps, "Lamp." The two translators I will compare and comment for this poem are Stephen Owen and Paula M. Varsano. For Owen, the poem does not say much more than "simply offer the pleasure of beautiful lines" (Owen, *Late Tang*, 474). Paula M. Varsano, instead, who translates the poem as an example of the rhetoric of hiddenness in her edited study on traditional Chinese culture,[15] finds that its sensual surface "is like a gleaming piece of obsidian. Neither transparent enough to serve as a window nor reflective enough to be a mirror, it irresistibly attracts the eye only to withhold any compensatory promise of vision" (Varsano 1). While for Owen the "Lamp" is just one of Li Shangyin's poems about a thing, for Varsano, the poem has deeper implications because she views the lamp as an instrument of light and hiddenness.

燈 Lamp

皎潔終無倦 Bright and pure, always tireless
煎熬亦自求 Burning and heating, also its own pursue
花時隨酒遠 In blooming seasons, it travels far with wines
雨後背窗休 After rains, it rests behind a window
冷暗黃茅驛 Dim and cold, at a mail stop in withered speargrass
暄明紫桂樓 Bright and warm, in a mansion of purple cassia
錦囊名畫掩 It sees famous paintings in their brocade bags

玉局敗棋收 It witnesses defeated pieces removed from the jade board
何處無佳夢 It seats where there is no good dream
誰人不隱憂 It shines as no one does not have hidden worries
影隨簾押轉 Its shadow turns following the curtain weights
光信簟文流 Its light flows along the mattress patterns
客自勝潘岳 The guest himself is better than Pan Yue
儂今定莫愁 I, today, must be Mourn-No-More
固應留半焰 Surely half flame shall be kept for later
回照下幃羞 to shine on the shyness when bed curtains are put down

(Translated by Pengfei Wang)

As expected, Varsano in her interpretation of this poem gives a more detailed line by line analysis of the poem to determine its hidden 情*qing* which, "depending on its immediate context, has engendered a range of definitions and translations, from 'truth' to 'emotion', with the latter being most closely associated with the world of literature" (Varsano 4). With the aim of searching for the hidden elements in Li's poetic enterprise, she finds that this poem is actually a combination of sources "as those found in the working of *yongwu* (詠物 poetry on things), the erotic atmospherics of the '*Ziye*' songs (子夜歌 midnight songs) of the Southern Dynasties, and even the earliest hermeneutic practices found in the *Shijing* and *Chuci*" (Varsano 12).

As Varsano points out, the word "Lamp" is never mentioned in the poem and if we did not know the title, we would not be able to read the poem. In fact, the poem is close to being an enigma and challenges the reader to guess what is the "Thing" being described. The lamp, she writes, is both an object of perception, even "an objet d'art" – and an agent that "illuminates other objects of perception: a mediator of observation" (Varsano 6). In other words, the lamp functions as a sign, or a trope, that signifies both itself and other signs.

The lamp is located in a room, and is "always tireless" in its brightness and purity. During the blossoming season, people may hold lamps to look at flowers during a night banquet, which is a reference to the well-known poetic motif of *carpe diem*: holding lights for night entertainment, because life is too short. Thus, a lamp "travels far with wines." On rainy nights, people go to sleep early and the lamp may "rest behind a window." Lamps can be found everywhere: in the "dim and cold," in shabby rural mail stops, as well as in the "bright and warm" luxury urban hotels.

Lamps, in an art collector's house, also have the chance to see famous paintings, which are rarely shown to the public and are, usually, carefully stored in brocade bags. Lamps in a chess master's house have probably watched many chess games played by the chess master, on the jade chessboard, and who sometimes lost. The lamp is also a witness of those who are asleep and dreaming, but also of those who are awake, and suffering. The lamp is also a witness of erotic encounters but always discreetly as it projects only the shadows of the lovers as they lower "the curtain-weights" of the bed, and as it follows them with its light along "the mattress patterns." The poem depicts the delicate play of light and shadow that makes it possible to capture or shed enough light to hide the indiscreet parts of the bedroom.

Four lines from the end, however, the poem takes a "baffling" turn from its descriptive mode, and addresses the reader in the first person: "the guest himself is better than Pan Yue / I, today, must be Mourn-No-More." Pan Yue was a very talented poet but was also known, in his lifetime, as very handsome, the most handsome man of his time.[16] Mo Chou, literally Mourn-no-more, on the other hand, is a fictional character, a character of local lore but also famous for her beauty.

There have been many attempts at explaining the meaning of this narrative shift as well as the identity of the speaker who introduces the guest, as well as who the guest may be, who is even more handsome than Pan Yue. Varsano believes that the speaker has entered a dream state that makes possible "the most dramatic transformation of the poem" (Varsano 11), namely, the speaker of the poem becomes a she, that is, Mourn-no-more, and addresses her guest as being more handsome than the poet Pan Yue.

However, it is only when we know that the title of the poem is "Lamp," we realize that it has only been a play of light and shadow, of hiddenness and revelation, as Varsano suggests. Then we also know that it has all been an illusion, brought about by the play of light of the lamp. The light of the lamp suggests the story of the art collector and the renowned paintings wrapped in brocade bags, and the story of the defeated chess master from the pieces left on the jade chessboard; but also the possible tragic love stories: stories of sleepless nights, and of suffering for love. The light of the lamp also makes it easy to see that the new guest is more handsome than Pan Yue by the light that it shines on him. It is all a question of light and darkness.

The poem does not end here; it continues to a final couplet:

> Surely half flame shall be kept for later
> to shine on the shyness when bed curtains are put down.

The lines have usually been read in relation to similar lines by Ji Shaoyu紀少瑜, a Liang Dynasty poet who lived around AD 541, who wrote: "I shall keep one or two candle-lights, so that I can see when I loosen your gown. 惟餘一兩焰，才得解羅衣." Commentators have seen the same sense of intimacy and sexual implication in Li Shangying's lines: "keep half the light burning," and wait to see "the shyness when she lowers the bed curtain." However, I do not think that this is what Li Shangyin meant to say. On the contrary, he is stating the opposite. One should keep the flame of the lamp low, "half-burning," to be discreet and in order not to shine directly on the "lowered bed-curtains."

What is at stake in the poem, in other words, is not erotic desire, or eternal desire, as Varsano claims, but only the illusion created by the lamp: these are the stories of the art collector and his famous paintings that we imagine from seeing the brocade bags; or the story of the defeated chess master that we can imagine from the pieces left on the jade chessboard, or, finally, a love story taking place behind "lowered bed-curtains." In actual fact, all there is in the room are these simple objects (a brocade bag, chess pieces and a lowered bed curtain) on which the light of the lamp shines and makes these stories possible to the reader's imagination.

The poem is an allegory of how a poem (by Li Shangyin) is constructed: a few objects that suggest possible stories, but none of them definite or conclusive. A good example is the "Ornamented zither" which is composed of four stories, the story of Zhuangzi and the butterfly, and three apparently tragic love stories, which, to this day, continue to baffle the reader who tries to put the pieces of stories together into a coherent whole. Another name for the lamp is "poetry," which shines with its rhetorical light on different objects suggesting their different stories and, in the case of Li Shangyin, tragic love stories.

The lamp, the zither or the writing on a monastery wall, are all examples of Li Shangyin's Baroque poetics which is not symbolic or historical, but poetic and allegorical. As such, a hermeneutical approach that looks for meanings in his poems is always bound to fail because the light that shines from them, or the zither the poem plays, the writing or the inscription, leave no residue.

Notes

[1] The poets' names in translations that are spelled different with the modern standardized Pinyin spellings are all adjusted in this book. Hinton, David. *The Late Poems of Meng Jiao*, xiv.

[2] Wu, Fusheng. *The Poetics of Decadence*, (Albany: SUNNY Press. 1998), 77.

[3] Owen, Stephen. *The Poetry of Meng Jiao and Han Yu*, (New Haven: Yale University Press, 1975), 144.
[4] Frodsham, J. D. *New Perspectives in Chinese Literature*, (Canberra: Australian National University Press, 1970), 12-13.
[5] Wong, Tai-wai. "Toward Defining Chinese Baroque Poetry," 25-72.
[6] The original sentence in Chinese is from the *New History of Tang*新唐書. The English translation quoted here is from J. D. Frodsham's *The Poems of Li He*, (Oxford: Clarendon Press. 1970), xvi.
[7] We do not really know the exact causes of Li He's young death, but it was most probably because of health reasons. In his introduction to his translations of Li He, Frodsham mentions a Qing dynasty commentator, Yao Wen-hsieh姚文燮, who believed that Li He's death was "brought about by sexual dissipation." This is a possibility given the evidence provided by his poems, which hardly make Li He "into a pillar of domestic sobriety" Frodsham (The Poems of Li He, 1970), xv.
[8] The song is collected in the *New Songs from the Jade Terrace*玉臺新詠, an anthology of early medieval Chinese poetry of romantic or semi-erotic "palace style" (gongti宮體) poetry, which dates from the late Southern Dynasties period (420-589).
[9] The song is from the *New Songs from the Jade Terrace.*
[10] The original poem is from the *New Songs from the Jade Terrace*. It is quoted here from the third volume of the *Anthology of the Poems of Pre-Qin Han Wei Jin Southern and Northern Dynasties*先秦漢魏晉南北朝詩.
[11] Zhu, Ziqing. "The Chronicles of Li He," *Journal of Tsinghua University*, Beijing, 1935:4, 887-915.
[12] The line is from the poem, "Antique Style": "The Antique style is out of fashion./ The new style requires more effort./ All the girls in town wear hair one foot in height,/ not just mine is high." In Lu Guimeng's, *Lu Guimeng Ji*, in Qi Yusheng ed. *Zhonghua Wenxue Mingzhu Baibu*, 380.
[13] On Li Shangyin's biography see James Liu's *The Poetry of Li Shang-yin*, (Chicago: University of Chicago Press, 1969).
[14] For an account of Li Shangyin's relationships with Buddhist nuns I refer to James Liu's study.
[15] Varsano, Paula M. *The Rhetoric of hiddenness in Traditional Chinese Culture*, (Albany: SUNY Press, 2016), 1.
[16] 世說新語*A New Account of the Tales of the World* is a collection of 1,130 historical anecdotes and character sketches of some 600 celebrities who lived in the late Han and Wei–Jin periods from the second to the fourth century.

Chapter 3

Metaphysical and Mid-Late Tang Conceits

Derived from the Italian term *concetto* (concept), a poetic conceit is an unconventional, logically complex, or surprising metaphor whose delight is more intellectual than sensual. As a rhetorical device, it is usually an extended metaphor or allegory. A conceit forms an extremely ingenious or fanciful parallel between apparently dissimilar or incongruous objects or situations and often is so farfetched as to be absurd, in some cases turning into strained ornamentation. The *Princeton Encyclopedia of Poetry and Poetics* describes conceit as follows: "all types of conceit share an origin which is specifically intellectual rather than sensuous. The poet compares elements which seem to have little or nothing in common, or juxtaposes images which establish a marked discord in mood." (Preminger 148)[1]

In classical Western poetry, there are usually two categories of conceit: Petrarchan and metaphysical. Petrarchan conceit came first to prominence in the fourteenth and fifteenth-century Renaissance literature when poets began using them in their imitation of the Petrarchan sonnet. In these poems, conceits were used most often to compare lovers to beautiful things in nature, but because of overuse and lack of innovation, over time, these conceits gained a negative connotation of being overdone. In the seventeenth century, the metaphysical poets greatly popularized the use of the device but they used conceits so extensively and so unrestrainedly that they were quickly criticized. Samuel Johnson in his "Life of Cowley" refused to accept the works of the metaphysical poets as poems and defined their use of conceits as wit that "abstracted from its effects upon the hearer," a combination of dissimilar images, or occult resemblances that may be more adequately defined a kind of "*discordia concors.*" (Johnson 51)[2]

Although Johnson's comments were unnecessarily negative, the conceits that we associate with Metaphysical poets are actually more intricate intellectual devices. Their conceits usually establish an analogy between one entity's spiritual qualities and an object in the physical world and control the whole structure of the poem. In a metaphysical conceit, writes Alex Preminger in the *Princeton Encyclopedia of Poetry and Poetics,* "the spiritual qualities or functions of the described entity are presented by means of a vehicle which shares no physical features with the entity" (Preminger 148). The metaphysical conceit characterizes less conventional and more esoteric associations, which are used to fuse the sensory and the abstract, trading on the element of surprise and the unlikeness to hold the reader's attention. Helen Gardener defines conceit as the "most immediately striking feature" of metaphysical poetry, which is "a comparison whose ingenuity is more striking than its justness, or, at least, is more immediately striking."[3] But the emotion evoked by the conceit is not limited to surprise but, according to Preminger, always entails "a surprised cognition of the ultimate validity of the relationship presented in the conceit, which thus serves not as an ornament but as an instrument of vision" (Preminger 149).

A metaphysical conceit is supposed to make sense intellectually rather than intuitively, because it is a blend of emotion and intellectual ingenuity that by strikingly comparing apparently unconnected ideas and things gets the reader startled out of his complacency and forces him or her to think through the argument of the poem. Metaphysical poetry is less concerned with expressing feelings than with analyzing them, therefore, a conceit will make sense only through the poet's complex argumentation. A good example is John Donne's famous conceit of "The Flea" which compares physical intimacy to a flea. The conceit makes sense only after the reader reads the argumentation that Donne makes in the poem.

The metaphysical poetry of the seventeenth century originated from the poetry of the preceding Elizabethan age without a major break. The typical Elizabethan poetry expressed comparatively simple and conventional themes in a style of conscious artifice and verbal elaboration, producing what Jack Dalglish calls, "mellifluous madrigals, charming love lyrics."[4] Moreover, the emphasis put on courtly love in poetry was also very indicative of the ideals followed by the Renaissance. Metaphysical poetry reacted against this idealized vision of love and opposed the "mellifluous sweetness" of courtly love by advocating a more realistic view in poetry (Fraser 87).[5] The metaphysical poets reacted against the stale conventions of the Elizabethan pastoral poets and sonneteers, explored the ramifications of their feelings and cast a new light on them from unexpected perspectives by finding connections between their feelings and intellectual concepts. Thus, metaphysical poetry became "a remarkable fusion of thought and feeling" (Dalglish 3), which is clearly crucial to the imagery of the metaphysical conceits that wanted to convey their feelings through "apparently" logical arguments. The imagery and conceit used in metaphysical poetry is not only for ornament or illustration, but it is also a means of communicating thoughts, exploring experience and finding new insights. Thus, the development of the conceit is also the development of the poet's thoughts.

Different from the Petrarchan conceit that was very popular with Renaissance writers of sonnets, the metaphysical conceit was a more intricate and intellectual device whose force rested not just in the unexpectedness of the image but also in how well the logical argument led the reader to respond emotionally in more appropriate ways. This characteristic is very evident in the poems of the three poets discussed here: John Donne, Andrew Marvell and Richard Crashaw. No matter how serious the basic theme of the poem, beside the blend of passion and thought, a self-expressive awareness of a variety of attitudes towards experience is always contained in the conceits themselves, which is not discovered until the reader grasps the whole argument of the poem.

An interesting view on metaphysical conceits comes from Katrin Ettenhuber's discussion of the metaphysical conceit in Donne.[6] She locates the origins of conceit in sixteenth and seventeenth-century rhetorical discourse by analyzing "the cultural and aesthetic assumptions" that underlie the reactions to the Metaphysical by Hazlitt and Johnson. She also turns to early modern approaches that do not make use of the term "conceit" but employ figures of speech like catachresis, "a stylistic transgression consisting of far-fetched, incongruous speeches." Catachresis is evidence of a mind "that must wander into the confines" and gravitates towards remote corners of the poetic map. She also deals with the topographical approach which emerges in Renaissance logic manuals.

Ettenhuber's discussion is useful when she claims that the metaphor "uniquely captures this register [as in Donne's Valediction poems] of grief and longing," and also "provides a temporary fiction of connectivity, as the lovers' minds converge in the remote logical places that constitute Donne's conceits" (Ettenhuber 393). However, her study of conceit, and catachresis, is limited to Renaissance manuals and examples from English Metaphysical poets but does not take into account theories of conceit and metaphor (catachresis is a mixed metaphor), which were also being discussed in Europe at the time. Theorists of the Baroque, as Emanuele Tesauro, as we see in the next discussion by Van Hook, also distinguished between conceits and metaphor, but went further to establish similarities between English Metaphysical poets and other Baroque poets.

Quite a different discussion on conceits comes from J. W. Van Hook whose perspective not only covers both English Metaphysical poets and European Baroque theory, but also attempts to establish similarities between the two.[7] For Van Hook, metaphysical poetry and Baroque poetry are synonymous, and Baroque poetics can provide insights to both metaphysical conceits and the worldview that the poetry expresses. He also differentiates between conceit and metaphor with the difference that "the conceit has its foundation in a rhetorical structure with unprecedented poetic and epistemological aims of its own" (Hook 24).

For Baroque theory, Hook turns to the work of Italian Baroque theorist, Emanuele Tesauro and his *Cannocchiale Aristotelico* (Aristotle's Telescope) (1654), for whom a conceit is a way of communicating between minds in order to by-pass questions of truth: "The object of a conceit is thus to communicate between the *ingegni* of the poet and his reader. It seeks to "relieve the listeners' minds in some way that will give them pleasure, without encumbering them with questions of truth"[8] (Tesauro 493, Hook 24). For Tesauro, the distinctive and peculiarly balanced structure of the conceit is designed to "delight the intellect with ingenious trains of thought" in order to absorb the audience wholly in some intransitive cognitive experience" (Tesauro 124, Hook 33).

The syllogism proper to the poetic conceit has its own distinctive form that corresponds to its need to remain "unencumbered by questions of truth." Tesauro calls it a "cavillous enthymeme" or "ingenious fallacy ... lacking the full syllogistic form," which further guarantees the autonomy of its witty conclusions by ambivalently "basing its middle term on some metaphor" (Tesauro 495, Hook 33). The full form of the Baroque conceit is thus a compound structure that includes both a metaphor and a fallacious argument built around it. Its two parts aim to engage the reader's judgment and imagination, simultaneously, to "seize the mind and excite it." What distinguishes the conceit, particularly, is its capacity to short-circuit the intellect's habitual guardian function, allowing the poet access to an imagination unencumbered by its customary obligations to truth and possibility.

According to Matteo Peregrini, the other major Italian Baroque theorist quoted by Van Hook, the conceit has the unparalleled power to surprise the mind on first encounter in such a manner that it cannot be a diligent judge of the things that the poet's images propose. "My goal," Peregrini writes, "is thus to liberate the *ingegno* from the need to always refer so strongly to whatever is the case. I want to inform it of the immense treasure which it has access to within the infinite realms man is capable of imagining"[9] (Peregrini 189, Van Hook 35). The notion of conceit in Tesauro and Peregrini holds the promise of new ways of experience. They express, according to Van Hook, the dissatisfaction that was widespread in the seventeenth century, both in England and on the Continent. He gives the example of John Donne's "Second Anniversarie," which speaks of the desire to "see all things despoyld of fallacies" (l. 295) and of fulfilling the rational faculty's latent potential by severing it from empirical experience and imagination:

> When will thou shake off this Pedantery,
> Of being taught by Sense, and Fantasy?
> Thou look'st through spectacles ... (ll. 291-93)

Impatient with the limitations imposed by these "spectacles," it is not surprising, comments Van Hook, that Donne should have produced as many examples of complex and elaborate rhetorical structures that Italian theorists identified as conceits.

Van Hook also quotes the witty enthymeme at the end of Donne's "The Good Morrow," as an example of true Baroque:

> What ever dues, was not mixt equally;
> If our two loves be one, or, thou and I
> Love so alike, that none doe slacken, none can die (ll. 19-21).

According to Van Hook, Tesauro's analysis can help us distinguish conceits from any of these simpler structures, just as it can plausibly suggest that a sort of *maraviglia* (wonder) might be our most appropriate response to the conceits we identify. Ultimately, for Tesauro, conceits drive the mind toward a new mode of awareness and vision until the readers, "as though themselves altered, strangely modify whatever they come to speak of, magnifying things, or coupling them together in new ways" (Tesauro 501, Hook 35). In particular, Van Hook stresses the importance and significance of Baroque poetics for readers of metaphysical poets. Theorists like Tesauro make it possible for us to distinguish fully elaborated conceits, and some of their epistemological assumptions, from mere instances of uncomplicated paradox, sophistry, or metaphor, which are merely the elementary components of those figures.

In "Delle acutezze, che altrimenti spiriti, vivezze e Concetti si appellano" (Witticisms which are also called spirits, liveliness of mind and conceits) (1639), Matteo Peregrini makes the point that this type of conceit not only seeks to create "wonder" ("maraviglia"), but also serves as a kind of arch, or bridge, which makes sure that what is being said "penetrates and impresses itself more boldly" on the reader's understanding.[10] For Van Hook, this is the distinguishing trait between Donne's style and that of Marvell and Herbert, who tend to absorb the reader's imagination in the poem's "marvelous" reality. However, all these poets are, for Van Hook, ultimately, similar. "They aim to stretch the epistemological capacities of the reader by exercising the mental faculties in unfamiliar ways." He also quotes Tesauro to the effect that "Ultimately conceits drive the mind toward a new mode of awareness and vision until the readers, "as though themselves altered, strangely modify whatever they come to speak of, magnifying things, or coupling them together in new ways" (Van Hook 38, Peregrini 127, Tesauro 90).

In conclusion, Van Hook claims that neither "the dayes rude hoarse minstralsey" ("Love's Alchymie," l. 22) nor the wild promptings of unbridled fantasy would win Donne's unqualified endorsement" (Hook 38). Donne's poems embody the fusion of intellect and imagination to which, in "The Crosse" he refers as man's corrected "concupiscence of witt" (l. 58). This poetic attitude is what confused Dr. Johnson when he reduced the metaphysical conceits to a mere image and which Baroque poetics "promises to make available to us once again" (Hook 38).

*****

As a rhetorical device, conceits are used in both Western and Eastern literature. According to one eminent Chinese critic, James Liu, "some later [Tang] poets resemble the Metaphysical Poets also in their use of far-fetched conceits, while earlier poets are generally content with comparisons that may easily occur to anyone."[11] By juxtaposing and manipulating images and ideas in esoteric ways, the poet invites the reader to a more sophisticated understanding of his objects of comparison, in which the poet uses one or more technique to effectively induce a desired effect on the reader, such as setting a mood or a point of view. A great deal of Mid-Late Tang poetry is allusive. A. C. Graham complains about the increasing allusiveness of Tang poetry, saying that "commentators illustrate nearly every line with quotations from older sources – standard references of mythological, historical, and geographical information, earlier examples of idioms, earlier uses of images which have accumulated special associations."[12] This is common in the Mid-Late Tang poetry, such as Li Shangyin's, in which images are the dominating factors while their allusions act as a secondary factor. Imagery in these poems, as James Liu points out, usually "involves a juxtaposition or a comparison of two objects, or a substitution of one object for another, or a translation of one kind of experience into another" (Liu, *Art of Chinese Poetry,* 102). In these cases, imagery has the double function of describing an immediate object and pointing at an analogy or contrast at the same time.

For the Chinese poets we are discussing (Meng Jiao, Li He and Li Shangyin), the An Lushan Rebellion (755-763) proved to be the watershed event that separated Mid-Late Tang poetry from its predecessors, and was responsible for turning its sublime and very formal imagery into a more subtle and gritty poetry. The imagery that had been an allusive device in the previous High Tang poetry became a target of poetic compositions and what had been the social function of poetry became a mean to convey "poetic ideas." Mid-Late Tang poetry placed emphasis on expressing the poets' psychological experiences by associating them with images that became more and more allusive. Stephen Owen, who like Dr. Johnson is not very fond of allusive poetry, call this new poetic lineage, a "technical poetics," because, according to him, "the poem begins with a quest for a *trouvaille*, a lucky find," and somehow finds it.[13] Li He's poetic practice, as Owen suggests, "challenged older notions of Confucian poetics and, instead of being a pure manifestation of the poet's sentiments or identity, the poem became a combination of good fortune and craft" (Owen, *Late Tang*, 113). It is hard to guess what Owen means by "good fortune" or whether his comment is also applicable to Meng Jiao and Li Shangyin. There is no "good fortune" in poetry but only craft. If the rhetorical devices that the poets use construct new ingenuous poetic visions this is not due to "good fortune" but to "good craft."

As a rhetorical device, conceits are also used in Baroque Mid-Late Tang lyric. At the level of theory, what has been said earlier of the conceits that are applicable to English Metaphysical poetry and to Continental seventeenth-century poetry also applies to Chinese Baroque poetry. However, while the scholarship on Western Baroque abounds, as we have seen, this is not the case with Eastern or Chinese Baroque. The label of "Baroque" to Tang poetry, as I have indicated, is a recent addition, therefore, the critical literature is minimal. Besides Frodsham, James Liu and Tak-wai Wong, who are the main proponents of Baroque in Tang poetry, the term is hardly mentioned in critical discussions of this period. In fact, this is the main objective of my study: not only to show that Mid-Late Tang poetry (namely, the poetry of Meng Jiao, Li He and Li Shangyin) can be read as Baroque poetry, but also that the way the term has been applied to these poets by Liu and Wong does not adequately do justice to their poetry.

In many ways, to speak of conceits in Mid-Late Tang poetry is to break new ground on the subject as there is no such a thing in Chinese literary criticism. On the contrary, there is a resistance to calling these poets, and others that I do not discuss, such as Han Yu (a patron and friend of Meng Jiao), Baroque. The situation is similar, to some extent, to what transpired in England with Dr. Johnson who called poets like Donne and Herbert "metaphysical" rather than "Baroque," as was the trend, then, in Europe, and chose to view their conceits as images, as Van Hook has reminded us in his discussion. The reason for this resistance is ideological and has to do with the way we define the Baroque. In Europe, at least, Baroque poetry, as I have indicated in the Introduction, was associated with allegory, a non-artistic mode, which opposed traditional, symbolic forms of art. In fact, the Baroque is defined by the way it departs from a symbolic mode of art. Where traditional or Renaissance forms of art went out of their way "to conceal art," namely, the rhetorical apparatus that made it possible, the Baroque poet went out of his way to emphasize a poem's rhetorical structure: the tropes that made it up. Whereas, traditional poetry gave the illusion that what was being portrayed was somehow related to reality, or had something to do with it, the Baroque poet went out of his way to shatter this illusion. While giving the illusion that he is describing reality, he also points out that any similarity leads to error. This particular characteristic of allegory made the Italian philosopher and literary critic Benedetto Croce wish that the Baroque was only confined to the seventeenth century, which he called the century "without poetry," because for him, poetry is only symbolic. He also believed that allegorical poetry was limited to the seventeenth century, and that poetry of other periods was immune from it. Allegory, in Croce's view, was a sign of disruption, error, confusion and obscurity, and most literary critics, East and West, have, similarly, a natural dislike for allegory.

As I indicated in the Introduction, Nietzsche was one of the few who, instead, defined the "Baroque" as a literary style that can be found in any period and in any place: in Continental Europe as well as in China. For Nietzsche, the Baroque is a necessary, if not inevitable, style which occurs in all art since the illusion of the symbol can only deceive so much and for so long. Art that conceals art is, after all, only a rhetorical construct and the referential illusion which it creates of imitating a world beyond art is only a deception. When poets tire of pretending that their art imitates reality they denounce the rhetorical nature of their imagery. Literary critics, however, both East and West, like to believe that art or literature is meaningful for life and that poets or artists imitate reality. Chinese scholars claim that Chinese poetry and art is essentially symbolic. For instance, Haun Haussy, in *The problem of a Chinese aesthetic*, claims that allegory is only a Western concept and that Chinese aesthetics identifies with the symbol.[14]

This is also true of those literary critics who are sympathetic to the Baroque like James J. Y. Liu and Tak-wai Wong. As I mentioned in the Introduction, James Liu was the first to write a study on Li Shagyin as a Baroque poet. Tak-wai Wong also wrote a lengthy essay on the Baroque where he is critical not only of Frodsham, who was the first to speak of Chinese Baroque for Tang poetry, but also of James J. Y. Liu. Despite their differences, Wong and Liu have a similar attitude toward the Baroque. They not only reject allegory as a viable poetic mode but they approach a Baroque poem as if it were a traditional, symbolic poem. They do not speak of conceits or try to identify them, they list elements that in their view characterize the Baroque, and that Chinese poems have in common with their English Metaphysical counterparts. When James Liu alludes to the conceits that Chinese poems may have in common with them, it is always in a general way, as when he states that "some later [Tang] poets resemble the Metaphysical Poets also in their use of far-fetched conceits, while earlier poets are generally content with comparisons that may easily occur to anyone" (Liu, *Art of Chinese Poetry*, 114). When dealing with allusion, which is the main trope of Li Shangyin's poetry, James Liu and Wong do not regard it as a conceit but as a far-fetched mannerism that creates obscurity rather than clarity. By juxtaposing and manipulating images and ideas in esoteric ways, they believe that the poet invites the reader to a more sophisticated understanding of his objects of comparison, so as to effectively induce a desired effect on the reader, such as setting a mood or a point of view. A scholar and translator like A. C. Graham, for instance, as I have indicated in my discussion of Li Shangyin's "Written on a Monastery Wall," is annoyed by the increasing allusiveness in his poetry and in Tang poetry, in general, which makes his work as a translator more difficult. He is annoyed that "commentators illustrate nearly every line with quotations from older sources – standard references of mythological, historical, and geographical information, earlier examples of idioms, earlier uses of images which have accumulated special associations."[15]

Since Chinese scholars and critics look at their English counterparts to develop their idea of Baroque, they ignore the theories of Tesauro or Peregrini, or of other continental critics of the Baroque who could provide a more comprehensive as well as allegorical understanding of the Baroque. It is inevitable, therefore that for them, we are dealing with images and not with conceits. So James Liu identifies images as the dominating factor in the poetry of Li Shangyin rather than tropes such as allusion. As he states, imagery in Mid and Late Tang poetry usually "involves a juxtaposition or a comparison of two objects, or a substitution of one object for another, or a translation of one kind of experience into another" (Liu, *Art of Chinese Poetry*, 102). Imagery is limited to the double function of describing an immediate object and of pointing to an analogy and to a contrast at the same time.

The conceits of Late-Tang poetry described in this study constitute a first in the history of Chinese literary criticism, where they have been defined with any criteria. However, the credit belongs to J. D. Frodsham, who was the first sinologist who suggested that Chinese literary history should be periodized according to the Western model. He felt that just as Chinese makes use of Western terminology in defining History to differentiate the medieval from modern and contemporary periods, they ought to do the same with literary history.[16] He thought that one should also be able to speak of Romanticism, Neo-Classicism, as well as Baroque in Chinese literature and Chinese literary history. Frodsham is the real pioneer of the study of Baroque in Mid-Late Tang poetry, even though he never wrote a study of Chinese Baroque.

The Conceits in English Metaphysical Poetry

John Donne

The Flea

The core conceit of the poem is the flea which has just bitten the poet and his lover. The flea's bite joins them as does sexual intercourse, so her chastity should no longer be an issue or should stop her from yielding to him. She should not feel guiltier for having sex with him than having the flea unite their blood with a bite. Sex itself is but a small pleasure: "Mark but this flea, and mark in this/ how little that which deny'st me is" (ll. 1-2), and should not be taken too seriously. The blood the flea extracts, as well as its final death, are symbols of love.

The flea was not Donne's invention. It was already a popular and widely used subject in erotic poems in the sixteenth century. Its popularity was celebrated in a publication of 1582, *La Puce de Madame de Roches*, a collection of poems on fleas in all the five major European languages: French, Spanish, Italian, Latin and Greek.[17] Besides their early popularity in the writings of the Roman erotic poet Ovid, popular view in the seventeenth century believed that fleas had a strong erotic association with sex because of the fleas' bloodthirsty nature and tendency to bite and drink blood from different people, and mix human blood in their bodies. The similarity makes the flea a good metaphor for lust. Donne exploits the metaphor to the fullest and turns it into one of the most famous conceits of metaphysical poetry, if not of the English language. In Donne, the conceit is used to persuade his lover to have sex with him before they are married. As the flea mingles the lovers' bloods inside its body, the lovers are already united "sexually," although she refuses to believe him that the mingling of their bloods is not "a sin, or shame, or loss of maidenhead." The poet's argument is that since blood is the essence of life, the flea spares three lives: besides their own two lives, there is also the flea's life. Inside the flea, the poet's and his beloved's blood constitute a relationship between them which is more than married, because the flea becomes their "marriage bed, and marriage temple." Despite his argument, she tries to kill the flea and succeeds. The poet reminds her that with the flea's death, she lost nothing except the drop of blood it sucked from her, and that, likewise, by having sex with him, she will not lose her honor except for those few drops of blood. All the fears that prevent her from yielding to him are misplaced, especially the fear of losing her honor that she fears most, because all she will lose is what "this flea's death" took from her.

The Good Morrow

The main conceit of the poem is the legend of the Seven Sleepers. Donne uses it to deal with the different spiritual states of the lovers before and after falling in love, when they wake up after a night of sleeping together. The Seven Sleepers' legend, as Redpath points out, is translated from the Syrian in Gregory of Tours' *De Gloria Martyrum* (Redpath 3) and relates that in AD 250 or 251 during the persecution of the Christians by Emperor Decius, seven Christian youths from Ephesus took refuge in a cave in a nearby mountain. Their pursuers walled up the entrance of the cave with the intention of starving them to death, but the young men fell into a miraculous sleep, from which they did not wake up until sometime during the reign of Theodosius II (possibly AD 439 or AD 446). When they did, they thought they had been asleep only for a single night, and one of them, who went to the city for food, was amazed to find the cross on churches and other buildings which, when he fell asleep, had been the object of desecration.

Donne uses the legend to strike a parallel between the seven youths who woke up to the new reality of a world dominated by the victory of Christianity, and the lovers who wake up to the victory of the miraculous joy of Love over sexual pleasure. Although the original legend has strong religious implications, Donne makes use of it for his own practical purposes. His main focus is the contrast between the different spiritual states of the lovers before and after they have slept together. Before waking up, the state of lovers' spirituality is childish and immature; after they wake up, their spirituality has grown, and they wake up to true love. True love makes them see the world differently: a world that will never die.

The Sun Rising

The main conceit is the personification of the sun – a "busy old fool" – whose business is to get everyone out of bed and on their way to work. The poet complains and rails against the sun because when the sun rises, it wakes him up and disturbs him when he is asleep with his beloved. He tells the sun to go annoy schoolboys and rush them to school, or to call on the huntsmen to prepare for the king's ride, or on the farmer to work in the fields. The lover's seasons do not change according to the sun but have their own pace, which is set by the lovers. The sun, which creates time, has no influence on love; in love there is no time.

The poet's argument with the sun generates most of the humor of the poem, especially, when he claims that he is stronger than the sun, because he can "eclipse and cloud" his beams just by blinking. At the end of the poem, the poet makes a deal with the sun. He does not have to shine on all the treasures of the world but just on him and his beloved because all the treasures of the world are there with them.

Andrew Marvell

To His Coy Mistress

The main conceit is the *carpe diem* motif: Time and Death will bring away their youth and beauty and, therefore, the mistress should yield to the poet and enjoy their love. To persuade her, the poet uses biblical references and the concept of vegetable love to exaggerate how long it would take if they waited, but this is all time they do not have. The motif of the winged chariot is also used to indicate how fast time runs. Time is fast and brief, therefore the mistress should not waste too much time by hesitating. Time will also affect his mistress' beauty. The poet would gladly give her all the years she needs to make up her mind and hopefully decide for him, if they had "world enough, and time." If he had time, he would admire every part of her beautiful body, praise her endlessly, accept her coyness, and even allow her to refuse him and wait for her for all eternity. But there is no time. The poem provides Marvell with the opportunity to show off all his scholarly knowledge. He makes use of the popular millenarian ideas of the seventeenth century to express the length of time that his mistress could take to overcome her hesitation and shyness. The biblical references go back to the Flood as recorded in Genesis in the *Old Testament*; to God's decision to return to earth and the "conversion of the Jews," as well as a reference to Christ's second coming. The concept of the vegetable in the tripartite soul is used to emphasize his view of time. The "vegetable love," literally, means that love is like a vegetable, a plant that will grow taller and taller and reach different parts of his mistress' body. However, since they do not have the luxury of thousands of years, the poet becomes impatient and tries to put pressure on her. He reminds her that as she grows old, her treasured virginity will only be loved by worms in her grave. She could save her virginity to the bitter end, but her life will be over before she knows it. He tells her that she would not lose any honor if they slept together, so it would be better to make the most of it and not waste any more time, while they are still in their prime. This is the typical leitmotif of *carpe diem*: seize the day and do not hold back, because beauty melts away and time elapses irrevocably.

The Definition of Love

The main conceits of this poem explore the nature of love. Marvell is concerned with the unattainability of "two perfect but irreconcilable" loves rather than the fulfillment of love through union, and focuses on the role of despair rather than hope, as in most other poems where, according to Nigel Smith, "hope usually precedes despair in descriptions of the progress of love."[18] This love, rather, is perfect and divine, and therefore unattainable. Personified Despair and Impossibility are the parents of this rarely born love, and Fate is the jealous obstructer. Perfect love of this kind is most unwelcome to Fate that never permits the union of perfect lovers. This love can be achieved only if three conditions are fulfilled: first, the spinning planets must collapse; second, the earth should be torn asunder by some new convulsion; and third, the whole world should be cramped or flattened into a planisphere. The allegorical status of these images is clear since they are all impossible to fulfill: perfect love cannot be fulfilled and the lovers cannot be united. The poet compares his love and that of his beloved to parallel lines that never meet. Just as only oblique lines meet in all geometrical angles, in the same way, only the passion of guilt or of adulterous lovers can be satisfied. Thus, this kind of perfect love can only achieve a spiritual union, never a physical one: "the conjunction of the mind, / And opposition of the stars."

The Unfortunate Lover

The main conceit is the unfortunate lover. The poem depicts the misfortunes that befell a lover who was unfortunate because he was the victim of a series of misfortunes, but he was also fortunate because only unhappy lovers become famous while the happy ones are soon forgotten. Marvell's allegory includes references to mythic imagery that establish a relation between the lover and the soul. The poem is one continuous metaphor which describes the inevitable suffering of the "time-bound soul," the lover's sacrifice and his redemption. The miserable sufferings of the unfortunate lover from the forced Caesarean section at his birth to his tragic death are an allegory of the unfortunate lover's soul and of his fate. As Nigel Smith writes, "the unfortunate lover's career in the world of passion corresponds to the temporal life of the soul" (Smith 76).

Richard Crashaw

To the Noblest and the Best of Ladies, the Countess of Denbigh

The main conceit of the poem is the parallel between spiritual rebirth and the delivery of the Countess'soul, who is being persuaded to convert to the Catholic faith, and her hesitation to opening her heart. Conversion is like a rebirth for the soul aspiring to convert; the soul is in labor, in the sense that only her own efforts can make it happen. The main allegory is of a trembling heart halting at the gate of bliss, as the Countess' doubts are said to be "Twixt Life and Death." Crashaw describes the spiritual state of the Countess, before making a decision, as a state of paralysis of the will, where any hesitation can be fatal. The longer she delays, the more pain she will suffer, as she is prolonging the birth pains of her soul. The habit of delay is her foe: "To save your Life, kill your Delay."

An Epitaph upon Husband and Wife

The main conceit of this poem is death as the second wedding and the grave as the second marriage bed. As the couple is buried together, their death is their second wedding and Death is the host officiating at the ceremony. The grave becomes their second marriage bed, where they can enjoy the love that will bind them forever. Fate may force the lovers to die physically by separating their bodies and souls, but it cannot deny their marriage because the lovers took vows before God and lived together in "one life." One should not weep for their physical death, because their souls are not dead; they have just fallen asleep.

The lovers are like turtles covered in their shells lying together and sleeping in the same grave: this is the last bond with which love can bind the two souls. Although the grave is not comfortable, the stone pillow hard and the sheets are cold, it is safe because "love made the bed" for them. When the stormy night ends and the pathos is gone, eternal life will come. And the couple will wake and rise from their dark grave to the heaven where there is no night and no death.

The Flaming Heart

The main conceit of the poem is the representation of the martyrdom of Saint Teresa in a painting or in poetry, between her painterly and the verbal representations. Crashaw's point is that the painting does not record faithfully the events of her death. The painter has mistaken the mysterious experiences described in her autobiography and has portrayed her as a weak, pale, faint female dwarfed by the bright, male Angel standing beside her. Crashaw gives the correct version of the scene and highlights the bodily desire of the saint to show her love for God and God's loving response in her transcendental ecstasy. The religious ecstasy is symbolized by "the Hand of this great Heart," which felt as if a Dart was thrust into Saint Teresa.

Crashaw's version of the painting entails a reversal of the traditional gender roles of masculine strength and feminine weakness. He writes: "Give him the veil, give her the dart." The poet addresses the saint in the first person and tells her that her love is so strong and ardent that she arouses a similar emotive response in him. He describes the "mysteries" of Saint Teresa's ecstatic rapture as the "Lights and Fires," "eagle in thee," "lives and deaths of love" and large "thirsts of love." The final lines of the poem describe Saint Teresa as the vehicle to achieve eternal life, just as reading the poem, rather than looking at the painting, is an inspiration to model one's own life on the life of Saint Teresa.

Metaphysical Themes

John Donne's "The Flea" takes the form of an erotic, humorous narrative. The predominant theme is the seduction of his lover that is brought about through the conceit of the flea. The strikingly original conceit of the flea is used to demonstrate that the two lovers are already united because the flea has bitten both their bodies and has mixed their blood. The poet wants to convince his lover that surrendering her virginity would be no shame under the sanctified circumstances provided by the flea. The tone of the poem is highly ironic, dramatic and quite amusing. The poem is a parody of the declarations of love and devotion typical of traditional love poetry. In their place, the poet offers philosophical and theological arguments that aim to persuade her that their union has already been consummated within the flea's little body. The poem wonderfully exemplifies Donne's confident and finely skilled rhetoric that makes a mockery of such an important subject and related high ideals. Donne's wit is illustrated by his ability to embody sexual desire, sin, sacred love and holy marriage in the body of a flea, before the woman finally kills it. The flea means nothing at all; just as losing her virtue means nothing at all. "The Flea" is a rhetorical tour de force, which, in an apparently simple poem, turns an entire tradition of love poetry on its "Baroque" head.

John Donne's poems contain several themes that frequently appear in his love lyrics, such as the lovers as a microcosm and neo-platonic love. These themes are found in "The Good Morrow" and "The Sun Rising," which incorporate Renaissance notions of the human body as a microcosm and lovers as constituting an entire world unto themselves. During the Renaissance, it was believed that the human body was a microcosm that mirrored the macrocosm of the world and universe. According to this view, the intellect governs the body, much like the king or queen governs the land. Donne employs this conceit to imply, instead, that the lovers' bodies contain the whole world, since they are so enamored with each other that they believe they are the center of the world and that nothing else matters but them. In "The Sun Rising," the poet tells the sun to shine exclusively on him and his beloved and, in so doing, the sun will shine on the entire world. Donne also draws on the Neo-platonic conception of physical and spiritual love as being two manifestations of the same impulse, and employs the concept in most of his love poems. In "The Good Morrow," for instance, Donne compares the lovers to the Seven Sleepers in the cave to the time before the lovers awake to true spiritual love. In this poem, John Donne brings together the subject of love and religion so that his love poetry becomes imbued with religious images and meanings.

The other major theme of Metaphysical poetry is death, which is one of Andrew Marvell's favorite themes and is at the center of his most famous poem, "To His Coy Mistress," where death is the logical premise of the *carpe diem* motif, and the main mode of persuasion used by the poet to seduce his mistress. In "The Definition of Love" the main theme is time, but the poet, as Ann Berthoff suggests, is mainly concerned with defining love "by the natural condition of temporal being."[19] In "The Unfortunate Lover," the theme of death is the premise of all the conceits of the poem: the paradisiacal garden, the storming sea, the tragic battle against Fortune, and the final apotheosis. The imagery of the battle against Fortune, one of the principal tropes, serves as the dramatic analogue, although, as Berthoff points out, "it appears largely as decorative reinforcement rather than dramatic metaphor" (Berthoff 83). The unfortunate lover is doomed to fail and die in the battle, because his death is an essential premise of his apotheosis at the end of the poem: "Yet dying leaves a perfume here, / And music within every ear: / And he in story only rule, / In a field sable a lover gules."

The same combination of religious devotion and spiritual love, and a concern with the theme of love in death is found in Richard Crashaw's "An Epitaph upon Husband and Wife," where death is said to be a second marriage. More typical of Crashaw are his erotic-religious poems, "The Flaming Heart" and "To the Countess Denbigh," where religious enlightenment becomes a form of sexual ecstasy. In these poems, there is a parallel between spiritual fulfillment derived from religious enlightenment and sexual pleasure. In "The Flaming Heart," Crashaw hopes that his poem on Saint Teresa can light a fire in his cold heart and lead him along a similar mystical path, up to the total annihilation of his self. In "The Letter to the Countess Denbigh," the poet invokes God as if He were Cupid and implores Him to find the arrow that could open the countess' heart. The poem concludes with an exhortation to the Countess to succumb to God's Love, which echoes the conventions of traditional love poetry: Love lays siege to her heart and to the fort of her "fair self."

The Conceits in Mid-Late Tang Poetry

The social circumstances that affect the poetry of the Tang poets discussed in the study are very different from those of the metaphysical poets. Meng Jiao, the first of the three Tang poets, is one of the leading figures of the trend "return to the antique." His poetry shows a moral seriousness and artistic self-consciousness, which was at the core of what Confucius saw as the didactic function of literature, which had been weakened by the popularity of the military heroism of the High Tang. The "return to the antique" focuses on the great social changes and political events that occurred in the second half of the eighth century which, as Stephen Owen observes, made Mid-Tang intellectuals like Meng Jiao, "less ambivalent and gave their allegiance more exclusively to traditionally Chinese social and moral values."[20] The ethical focus of Meng's poetry conformed to the high moral standards of the past that were highly regarded and to which he tried to return. The "ruggedness" of Meng Jiao's poetry seems to have approximated the poems of the *Book of Songs*, by comparison to the smooth, balanced parallelism of High Tang regulated verse. Even this analysis does not do justice to Meng's poetry. As Owen states, Meng Jiao carried this raggedness to such an extreme that "his poetry was felt to be more 'ancient than others'" (Owen, *Meng Jiao and Han Yu*, 18). Besides his departure from the poetry of his predecessors in the High Tang, Meng developed a personal style with several notable characteristics that distinguish him from his contemporaries. Owen lists them as: the use of unusual words and images to startle the reader; a tendency for hyperbole showing both cleverness of conceit and awkwardness; a tendency to speak in absolutes, in terms of "all" or "none," which in his later poetry allows the poet to make his "absolute" ethical judgments; a strong ethical position by which he evaluates all phenomena in terms of good and evil; finally, moral and ethical metaphors, which are used to heighten moral qualities and evaluate distinctions. (Owen, *Meng Jiao and Han Yu,* 24) In the three poems discussed here, these traits are very easily detected. The landscapes in "Cold Creek" and "Laments of the Gorges" are startlingly allegorical to represent the imbalance of the natural world by contrast to the cosmic order. In "Autumn Thoughts," the poetic logic of Meng's world is perfectly developed as many different worlds are made to coexist in one allegorical narrative.

Meng Jiao

Cold Creek III

As the title of the poem indicates, this is the third of a series of nine poems placed together in a narrative. The main conceit of Poem III illustrates the general barren and unusual early spring coldness which is common to all the poems. The frozen waves, the abandoned feathers, the frozen blood, the ghostly village of thorns and brambles, communicate the sense of a world which is dark, bitter and in decay. The macabre deaths of the fish and the birds are the poet's way of denouncing the disastrous age he lives in and the poor people like him who are made to suffer.

Autumn Thoughts VI

The poem is the fourth of a narrative of fifteen poems linked by a common theme. The main conceit of this poem is the moonlight which, unlike the romantic and friendly moon of Li Bai, has knife blades and a sword. This moon, instead of warming the poet's soul, freezes it, by reminding him of his remaining life. The moonlight sheds light on the foulness of the world and appears to wash it clean, but this is only an illusion. The poem is an allegory of the impossibility of poetry to whitewash reality and to give a romanticized and illusory view of the world. Like the moonlight, poetry can only provide the illusion of a better world, but this illusion is also denounced as an error.

Laments of the Gorges III

The poem is the third of a series of ten poems whose main conceit is the personification of the distorted landscape of the Gorges that reflect the poet's own inner self. The Gorges are the recipients of the memories of people and events that took place there and who now address the poet as an "exile" who has finally found his home in these gorges, which is also the end of the line for him.

Li He

Li He was one of the most imitated Mid-Tang poets for his ironic style of poetry, which disregarded traditional poetic forms. His poems are filled with macabre as well as sensual imagery, with an obsession for the eroticism of the Southern Dynasties Palace Style poetry, and for themes of impossible and tragic love. The "Song of Heyang," which is not about a place named "Heyang," is about the impossibility of love, about lovers who meet years later, and are now indifferent and stranger to each other. Some of his other poems are famous for the emphasis they place on sensuality and eroticism, and for the love and death theme. In "Su Xiaoxiao's Tomb," the irony of the poem consists in the discrepancy between an apparently natural landscape and the tomb where the famous prostitute Su Xiaoxiao rests. As she believed that even in death, she would wait for her lover, Li He's irony makes clear that even in death, one waits in vain. The poet is at his best when rewriting typical Palace Style poetry, apparently imitating the genre but subtly subverting it. This is the case of the other poem, "Song: A Lovely Girl Combing Her Hair." In this version, the woman in her morning ritual of doing her hair is no longer young and is no longer the object of admiration. After her usual, lengthy routine to do her hair, she has no other expectation than going in the garden alone to pick a spray of cherry blossoms.

Song of Heyang

This poem, like the next two, takes as its premise a traditional poem that provides the poet with the freedom to express his own poetic view. The title, "Heyang Song," refers to Heyang, a location north of the Yellow River. Usually, in traditional Chinese poetry, poems that have titles after places describe some event or some lore about the place, but this is not the case with this poem. It is typical of Li He to take up a traditional form and turn it into whatever subject he likes.

The main conceit of the poem is given in the first line: "When you dye silk clothes/Autumn blue is a difficult shade to get." This is the conceit of the dyed cloth to indicate that feelings between lovers do not develop easily, but require time and communication. Most often lovers do not always come together, as one never gets the shade of blue one desires. Critics are divided as to whether the poem is about the poet's personal experience or someone else's. The question does not affect the reading of the poem since it is clear that the person is now old and the girl he was in love with is still working as a singing girl in a state-run entertaining house. Once they were madly in love, now the man sees her at a performance. They do not sit together, but apart from each other, although he believes she must have seen him as well. The poem illustrates the initial conceit that "Autumn blue is a difficult shade to get," but the poem is also ironic because "autumn blue," can also be understood as a pun on "autumn" as a late stage in life. The feeling of loss and sadness that the man feels about a love affair that could have been, is only realized too late, in the "autumn" of his life.

Su Xiaoxiao's Tomb

This poem is also ironic in that it tells the story of Su Xiaoxiao, a famous prostitute and a very good singer who died young of an illness. Li He uses many of the conceits associated with her life story but gives his own personal version. The main conceit is the "oiled sides coach" which was a symbol of Su Xiaoxiao and which becomes in Li He's poem her tomb, as people at the time believed. The other conceit is the "true love knot," knotted with two laces or belts, which is said to be the symbol of undying love but it is also a euphemism for sexual intercourse in erotic literature. In the Tang dynasty, there was a version of this story that on stormy nights, when people went by her tomb, they could hear the sound of music and her singing coming from the tomb. This was a popular song whose theme was that true love can only be found after death, in the tomb. Although it is said that Li He never visited her tomb, in his version of Xiaoxiao's story, she waits for her lover in vain, because for Li He not even in death one can find true love. Death is the supreme irony.

Song: A Lovely Girl Combing Her Hair

The main conceit of the poem is a woman doing her morning toilet. The poem is based on a traditional Palace Style poem, which described women as precious toys. In Li He's version, the woman is only doing her hair, which in itself, is an arduous and lengthy task. His ironic take on this genre is to portray the woman as not in her prime and no longer beautiful. When she is finally done up and ready to go out to meet the men, there is no one waiting for her. She has spent hours doing her hair only to go alone in her garden to pick cherry blossoms.

Li Shangyin

Li Shangyin is perhaps unique in Late-Tang poetry because of the great variety of his poetic compositions, but also because of their allusiveness which gave him the reputation as a difficult poet. One major difficulty is that Li Shangyin, as James Liu has written, is a truly Baroque poet so that his poems cannot be read as if they were symbolic representations of real events. The best example is the "Ornamented Zither," in which, despite the beauty and sensuality of the images and the sense of loss conveyed by the poem, it is pointless to assign a definite meaning to all these images and allusions. The poem is not an imitation of the fifty strings zither of old but an allegory of the impossibility of ever coinciding with it. The poem does not bring about the recollection of youthful years because the tragic love stories to which the poem alludes leave the poet indifferent, because he is already "bewildered and lost." A similar poem, "Written on the Monastery Wall," apparently about Buddhism is, on close reading, a story of unfulfilled love of those Buddhist nuns who still feel the call of the flesh. The reference to the oyster's unfilled womb and the amber's desire for the pine are metaphors for their unfulfilled desires. The poem does not promote or denounce the practice of Buddhism but provides only an insight into a reality which the poet, most likely, was acquainted with.[21] The third poem, the "Lamp," is one of those poems about things where poets can write about any "thing" they like, like a "Lamp." However, when a poet like Li Shangyin writes about a lamp, it is never about a lamp, but, as in this case, the lamp becomes a symbol for poetry. Just as a lighted lamp in a room can suggest to the viewer's imagination stories about the people that occupied it, so does a poem about a lamp suggests stories about paintings left behind, defeats at chess, and a tragic love story. Figures of speech, tropes, are the light that the poem employs to shed light on these stories. Just like the light of the lamp only partly sheds light on the room, so the poet's language touches on the objects in the room discreetly, not stating but only suggesting.

The ornamented zither

The main conceit of the poem is the zither whose sound brings about the recollection of the poet's past, of his youthful years. However, the myths and the legends, which make up the recollection are all tragic love stories: Emperor Wang's love betrayal and death, and whose "spring heart" is entrusted to a cuckoo, the mermaids crying tears of pearls, the tragic love affair of Purple Jade who kills herself for love. In short, the poem makes clear that the poet's youthful years are not worth recollecting. These recollections do not lead to a knowledge of the past but only to confusion and bewilderment.

Written on a Monastery Wall

In this apparently religious poem on Buddhism, the main conceits of the oyster and the amber allude to Buddhist nuns, enclosed in the four walls of a Buddhist monastery, who still yearn for love and sexual fulfillment. The unfulfilled oyster and the unset amber symbolize their sexual desires that have not yet been hollowed by their faith.

Lamp

The poem belongs to a genre called "Poem on Things" which allows the poet to represent just any "thing" he likes. The main conceit is the lamp which sheds light and shadow on different objects in a room: paintings, a chess set, a bedroom. The lamp is a metaphor for the poem, which narrates the stories that these objects suggest to the poet's imagination. The "Lamp" describes how a poem creates the illusion of lived reality, how it generates stories from the objects or the things that catch the imagination of the poet. It is an allegory of a poem about a poem on "Things."

*****

From what has been said, it is clear that the Baroque styles of the English Metaphysical poets and Mid-Late Tang Poets differ somewhat even though they are formally the same. In their attempt to counter tradition with rhetorical innovations, metaphysical poets sought in conceits a way to maintain their poetic originality and personal freedom of expression. With the conceits of the Flea, the Seven Sleepers, and a humorous dialogue with the Sun, John Donne was able to express old ideas in new ways. Love is always the theme, both erotic and spiritual, but now it is couched in conceits that are no longer commonplace: the combining of blood in a flea to suggest a love bond and a marriage bed; the religious metaphor of the "Seven Sleepers" to suggest the radical difference between erotic and spiritual love; and the personification of the sun in "The Sun Rising" which rotates around the lovers solely for their benefit. The theme of love, or seduction, is found also in Andrew Marvell's "To His Coy Mistress." Here the old Renaissance motif of *carpe diem* is still at work. The shadow of mortality and the threat of running out of time make a powerful argument to seduce the unwilling mistress. The theme of death is also at work in "The Unfortunate Lover" where it becomes an instrument of redemption for the unfortunate lover, while in "The Definition of Love" the poet makes a plea for platonic love for the lovers whose parallel loves will never meet. Richard Crashaw, instead, is an example of religious poetry where the erotic and the spiritual seem to go hand in hand in "The Countess of Denbigh" and in the portrait of Saint Teresa in "The Flaming Heart." In "The Epitaph of a Husband and wife," death also makes its appearance where it is defined as a second marriage. What characterizes these metaphysical poems as Baroque is the way they make use of traditional Renaissance themes by re-presenting them in new ways, by breaking through the traditional and symbolic mold of their predecessors. They were castigated for their work by critics, but, today, they are admired for it, and we call them modern.

Love and death are not major themes of Mid-Late Tang poets but since they are universal themes, they find their way even in their poems. The significant difference between Metaphysical poets and Mid-Late Tang poets is that these work within an ancient poetic tradition which they make their own by modifying it or subverting it. In their poems, love is always tragic as we see in Li He's poems. His fascination with the Southern Dynasty Palace Style poetry makes him retell, in an ironic mode, the story of the prostitute Su Xiaoxiao and the legend that she will wait for her lover even in death, only to make the point that even then she will wait in vain. In "A Lovely Woman Combing Her Hair," modeled on a popular Palace Style poem, Li He portrays a woman who is past her prime, is no longer beautiful and no longer the object of men's attention. Her sadness, and tragedy, is understated in her picking a spray of cherry blossom. In "Song of Heyang" love between an older man and a woman is also an impossibility, and when years later they are together by chance, they have become strangers.

Love in Li Shangyin's poems is likewise tragic. In "The Ornamented zither," the music that reminds the poet of his youthful days is a recollection of tragic love stories. Even in an apparent religious poem like "Written on a Monastery Wall" the focus is on the tragic lives of Buddhist nuns who live behind monastery walls but still long for sexual fulfillment. Even in the "Lamp," the light which is cast on the bedroom curtains may hide an affair but also the loneliness of a lover who waits for someone who may never come.

The poems of Meng Jiao I have discussed seem to be the exception. Although love does not figure in these poems, tragedy is a constant theme which invests both the world of men and the natural world. The poems portray a desolate and decaying landscape, where death and corruption are the main themes. These poems were written late in life but, as he tells us in "Autumn Thoughts," he used to write a very different type of poems in his youth, which provided him with a better income. This poetry was vigorous but "it was empty discourse." Now his poetry is no longer "empty" but it is no longer successful, "Now my poetry declines – what can I rely on?" We do not know the type of poetry that Meng used to write in his youth and that he calls "empty," we only know that the type of poetry that he wrote late in life, such as "Cold Creek" and "Laments of the Gorges," are "meaning-full" and "no longer an empty discourse." We only know that while his late poetry did not provide him with a better income, his poems have guaranteed him a place in our modernity.

Notes

[1] Alex Preminger. *Princeton Encyclopedia of Poetry and Poetics (Enlarged Edition)*, (Princeton: Princeton University Press, 1974), 148.
[2] Samuel Johnson. "Lives of the Poets – Abraham Cowley (1779)," *The Metaphysical Poets: A Casebook*, edited by Gerald Hammond, (London: The MacMillan Press. 1974), 51.
[3] Helen Gardener. *The Metaphysical Poets*, (Harmondsworth: Penguin, 1982), xxiii.
[4] Jack Dalglish. *Eight Metaphysical Poets*, (London: Heinemann, 1963), 2.

[5] G. S. Fraser. *A Short History of English Poetry,* (Totowa: Barnes & Noble, 1981), 87.

[6] Katrin Ettenbauer. "Comparisons are odious? Revisiting the Metaphysical conceit in Donne," 393- 413.

[7] J. W. Van Hook. "Concupiscence of Witt": The Metaphysical Conceit in Baroque Poetics," 24-38.

[8] Emanuele Tesauro. *Il Cannocchiale Aristotelico* (1670).

[9] Matteo Peregrini. "Fonti dell' ingegno ridotti ad arte" (1650).

[10] Matteo Peregrini. *Delle Acutezze che Altrimenti Spiriti, Vivezze e Concetti si Appellano* (1639), I 18.

[11] James J Y Liu. *The Art of Chinese Poetry,* (Chicago: The University of Chicago Press, 1962), 114.

[12] A. C. Graham. *Poems of the Late Tang,* (Harmondsworth: Penguin Books, 1965), 27.

[13] Stephen Owen. *The End of Chinese "Middle Ages,"* (Stanford: Stanford University Press. 1996), 111.

[14] Haun Saussy. *The Problem with Chinese Aesthetic.* (Stanford, CA.: Stanford University Press, 1993).

[15] A. C. Graham. *Poems of the Late Tang,* 27.

[16] J. D. Frodsham. *New Perspectives in Chinese Literature.* (Canberra: Australian National University Press, 1970).

[17] Theodore Redpath. *The Songs and Sonnets of John Donne,* (London: Methuen. 1983), 175.

[18] Nigel Smith. *The Poems of Andrew Marvell,* (Harlow: Pearson Education, 2007), 107.

[19] Ann E. Berthoff. *The Resolved Soul: A Study of Marvell's Major Poems,* (Princeton: Princeton University Press. 1970), 106.

[20] Stephen Owen. *The Poetry of Meng Jiao and Han Yu,* (New Haven: Yale University Press, 1975), 3.

[21] On Li Shangyin's acquaintance with Buddhist nuns see *The Poetry of Li Shang-yin: Ninth-Century Baroque Chinese Poet,* (Chicago: University of Chicago Press, 1969).

Conclusions

The idea of working on the Baroque and of comparing Metaphysical poets and Mid-Late Tang poets came from reading James Liu's study on Li Shangyin as a baroque poet. I meant to expand his study to other poets, as Tak-wai Wong suggests in his study. I became aware, however, through Wong's critique of Liu and Frodsham, as well as from Wong's and Liu's analyses of how Chinese poets compare to Metaphysical poets, that their study did not provide a satisfactory model to analyze the Baroque characteristics of Tang poetry. Liu's and Wong's approach to baroque poetry is historical and not poetic, symbolic and not allegorical. They believe that the Baroque consists in a few elements that are characteristic of the genre but they discard the essential characteristic of the baroque as a poetic concept, namely, allegory. As I have shown, they approach an allegorical poem like Li Shangyin's the "Ornamented zither" as if it were a traditional and symbolic poem. They reject Frodsham's notion of Baroque which is indebted to Nietzsche's idea of Baroque as poetic style which can be found in different ages and cultures because what is baroque are not the specific devices a poet uses, which are common to any poetry, but a style of art which is predicated on the demystification of art as symbol.[1] This process of demystification occurs at any time in literary history, in the West as well as in the East, in Europe as well as in China, wherever, Nietzsche writes, "any great art starts to fade, whenever the demands in the art of classic expression grow too great." This is the path that I have followed in this study, in my analysis of English Metaphysical poets and Mid-Late Tang poets.

The main reason behind my study, however, was a desire to bring together Tang poetry closer to its Western counterparts, the English Metaphysical poets. James Liu's study on Li Shangyin's baroque poetry provided the idea that through comparative analysis one could establish a bridge between East and West, between the glorious epoch of Elizabethan England and the splendor of the Tang dynasty. The initial stimulus, however, came from J. D. Frodsham, the world-renowned sinologist and translator who had, as I mentioned in the Introduction, a similar desire not only to bring the East and West cultures together, but to even Westernize Chinese literary history. He believed that it would benefit Chinese culture and literature to describe the different Chinese literary stages on the Western model of literary history rather than in dynasties. This is where his idea of Chinese baroque poetry, or baroque Tang poetry, was born. He thought that this period of Chinese literary history, the ninth century, was comparable to the seventeenth century in the West. This was not just an educated guess. As a translator of Li He, and of other major poets of the Tang dynasty, he knew that these poets, like their English Metaphysical counterparts, had similarly moved away from traditional ways of doing poetry. In their poems, they did not attempt to provide an artistic representation, which could pass as symbolic of reality, but went out of their way to place emphasis on the devices and conceits that made possible for them to express their art, through which, nonetheless, they were able to communicate their vision of reality.

As a good reader of Chinese poetry, Frodsham understood that Chinese poets were doing what their counterparts did in other centuries. He knew that ninth-century Tang poetry was not very different from seventeenth-century English Metaphysical poetry, or from other forms of poetry in Europe that was called "Baroque." This conviction influenced the way he translated and interpreted Tang poetry. Most poems, translated by Chinese scholars in China, but also in the West, tend to be very literal, as translators try to give as close a rendition of the original as possible. While this is an acceptable procedure, the results are not equally satisfactory. In most cases, one gets a general idea of what the poem is about but it is difficult to understand it in its details. Frodsham's translations, however, are done with the Western reader in mind. He reads the poem as close as possible to the original, but in his final translation, he turns it into a Western poem. My knowledge of Chinese allowed me to see the difference between the two types of translations, which I have discussed in Chapter two on Mid-Late Tang poetry. I must say although I prefer Frodsham's translations to the more literal ones of the other translators, I created my own translations to deliver my interpretation of the poems. Where I have not followed Frodsham is in his attempt to turn Chinese literary history into Western literary history. I think we are fine as we are.

Notes

1 Friedrich Nietzsche. "On the Baroque style." *Human, All too Human. A Book for free spirits,* Translated by R. J. Hollingdale. Introduction by Richard Schacht. (Cambridge: Cambridge University Press, 1986, 1996), 245-46.

Works Cited

English Metaphysical Poets. Primary Sources:

Avila, Saint Teresa of. *The Life of Saint Teresa of Jesus.* Trans. David Lewis. London: T. Baker, 1904. Print.

Dalglish, Jack. *Eight Metaphysical Poets.* London: Heinemann Educational Books. 1963. Print.

Donne, John, and John T Shawcross. *The Complete Poetry of John Donne.* London: University of London Press, 1968. Print.

Gardner, Helen. *The Elegies and The Songs and Sonnets.* Oxford University Press, 1965. Print.

___________. *The Metaphysical Poets.* Oxford: Oxford University Press, 1967. Print.

Preminger, Alex, ed. *Princeton Encyclopedia of Poetry and Poetics (Enlarged Edition).* Princeton: Princeton University Press. 1974. Print.

Redpath, Theodore. *The Songs and Sonnets of John Donne. Second edition.* London: Methuen. 1983. Print.

Rumrich, John P. and Chaplin, Gregory. Eds. *Norton Critical Edition of Seventeenth Century British Poetry: 1603-1660,* New York: W.W. Norton & Company, 2006. Print.

Smith, Nigel. *The Poems of Andrew Marvell.* Harlow: Pearson Education. 2007. Print.

Williams. G. W. *The Complete Poetry of Richard Crashaw* (1631-1649). New York: New York University Press, 1972. Print.

*****

Mid-Late Tang Poetry. Primary Sources:

*Anthology of the Poems of Pre-Qin Han Wei Jin Southern and Northern Dynasties*先秦漢魏晉南北朝詩. Vol. III. Liqin Lu, Beijing: Zhonghua Shuju Press. 2006, 1953. Print.

*A New Account of the Tales of the World*世說新語. Print.

李賀著, 王琦等評註, 三家評註李長吉歌詩. 上海：上海古籍出版社. 2011. Print.

劉學鍇, 余恕誠 著, 李商隱詩歌集解. 北京：中華書局. 1988. Print.

陸龜蒙, 陸龜蒙詩歌全集, 齊豫生編中華文學名著百部, 烏魯木齊：新疆青少年出版社, 2000. Print

孟郊著, 夏敬觀, 王雲五編, 孟郊詩. 台北：商務印書館. 1940. Print.

孟郊著, 華忱之編, 孟東野詩集. 北京：人民文學出版社. 1959. Print.

陆龟蒙著, 陆龟蒙诗集. 中华文学名著百部, 齐豫生, 夏于全主编. 乌鲁木齐：新疆青少年出版社. 2000. Print.

*New History of Tang*新唐書. Print.

*New Songs from the Jade Terrace*玉臺新詠. Print.

*****

Translations and commentary of Mid-Late Tang poems in English:

Cooper, Arthur. *Li Po and Tu Fu.* London: The Penguin Classics, 1973. Print.

Graham, A. C. *Poems of the Late Tang.* Harmondsworth: Penguin Books, 1965. Print.

Hinton, David. *The Late Poems of Meng Jiao.* Princeton: Princeton University Press, 1996. Print.

Owen, Stephen. *The Late Tang. Chinese Poetry of the Mid-Ninth Century (827-860).* Harvard University Asia Centre. Cambridge (Mass.) and London: Harvard University Press, 2006. Print.

*****

Mid-Late Tang Poetry. Secondary Sources:

Ash, Michael B. "The Tu Mu and Li Shang-yin Prefaces to the collected poems of Li Ho." *Studies in Chinese Poetry and Poetics.* Print.

Frodsham, J. D. *New Perspectives in Chinese Literature.* Canberra: Australian National University Press, 1970. Print.

__________. *The Poems of Li He (791-817).* Oxford: Clarendon Press. 1970. Print.

Liu, James J Y. *The Art of Chinese Poetry.* Chicago: The University of Chicago Press, 1962. Print.

_________. *The Poetry of Li Shangyin: Ninth-Century Baroque Chinese Poet.* Chicago: University of Chicago Press, 1969. Print.

Owen, Stephen. *The Poetry of Meng Jiao and Han Yu.* New Haven: Yale University Press, 1975. Print.

___________. *The End of Chinese "Middle Ages": Essays in Mid-Tang Literary Culture.* Stanford: Stanford University Press. 1996. Print.

__________. *The Late Tang. Chinese Poetry of the Mid-Ninth Century (827-860).* Harvard University Asia Centre. Cambridge (Mass.) and London: Harvard University Press, 2006. Print.

Saussy, Haun. *The problem with Chinese aesthetic.* Stanford, CA.: Stanford University Press, 1993. Print.

Varsano, Paula M. *The Rhetoric of hiddenness in Traditional Chinese Culture.* Albany: SUNY Press, 2016. Print.

Wong, Tak-wai. "Toward Defining Chinese Baroque Poetry," *Tamkang Review 8,* No.1, 1977, 25-72. Print.

Wu, Fusheng. *The Poetics of Decadence: Chinese Poetry of the Southern Dynasties and Late Tang Periods.* Albany: SUNNY Press. 1998. Print.

Zhu, Ziqing. "The Chronicles of Li He," *Journal of Tsinghua University*, Beijing, 1935:4, 887-915.

*****

General Secondary Sources:

Augustine, Saint. *Confessions.* Translated with an Introduction by R. S. Pine-Coffin. Penguin Books, 1961. Print.

Benjamin, Walter. *The origin of German tragic drama.* London: Verso. 2009. Print.

Berthoff, Ann E. *The Resolved Soul: A Study of Marvell's Major Poems.* Princeton: Princeton University Press. 1970. Print.

Bloom, Harold. *John Donne: Comprehensive Research and Study Guide.* Broomall: Chelsea House Publisher, 1999. Print.

Borges, Jorge Luis. *A universal history of infamy.* New York: Dutton, 1978. Print.

Croce, Benedetto. *Storia dell'eta Barocca in Italia.* Pensiero, poesia e letteratura e vita morale. Bari: G. Laterza, 1957. Print.

Dalglish, Jack. *Eight Metaphysical Poets.* London: Heinemann, 1963. Print.

De Man, Paul. *Aesthetic Ideology.* Minneapolis: University of Minnesota Press, 1996. Print.

____________. *Blindness and Insight,* Minneapolis: University of Minnesota Press, 1983. Print.

De Mourgues, Odette. *Metaphysical Baroque and Precieux Poetry.* Oxford: Oxford University Press, 1953. Print.

Dryden, John. "A Discourse of the Original and Progress of Satire." Ed. Watson (1962), 2: 144. Online.

Eliot, T. S. "The Metaphysical Poets" in *Selected Prose of T. S. Eliot.* New York: Harcourt Brace Jovanovich, 1975. Print.

Ettenhuber, Katrin. *Donne's Augustine: Renaissance cultures of interpretation.* Oxford: Oxford University Press. 2011. Print.

Finn-Atkins, Alexandra. *The Redemptive Act of Reading: Richard Crashaw and the Tersean Liturgy.* Thesis. Providence College, 2012. Print.

____________. "'Comparison are odious'? Revisiting the Metaphysical Conceit in Donne". *The Review of English Studies.* New Series. Vol. 62, no. 255 (June 2011), 393- 413. Print.

Fraser, G. S., *A Short History of English Poetry.* Totowa: Barnes & Noble, 1981. Print.

Grady, Hugh. *John Donne and baroque allegory: the aesthetics of fragmentation.* Cambridge: Cambridge University Press. Print.

Grierson, Herbert, J.C. and Fowler, Alastair. *Metaphysical Lyrics and Poems of the Seventeenth Century: Donne to Butler.* Oxford: Oxford University Press, 1928. Print.

Hegel, G. W. *Lectures on Fine Art.* Oxford: At the Clarendon Press, 1975. Print.

Hirst, Derek, and Zwicker, Steven. "Eros and Abuse: Imagining Andrew Marvell," *ELH*, Vol. 74, No. 2 (Summer, 2007), 371-395. Print.

Hitrat, Husain. *The Mystical Element in the Metaphysical Poets of the Seventeenth Century*. Edinburgh: Oliver and Boyd, 1948. Print.

Hook, J. W. van. "'Concupiscence of Witt': The Metaphysical Conceit in Baroque Poetics," *Modern Philology*, Vol. 84, No. 1 (Aug., 1986), 24-38. Print.

Johnson, Samuel. "Lives of the Poets – Abraham Cowley (1779)," Gerald Hammond ed. *The Metaphysical Poets: A Casebook*, London: The MacMillan Press. 1974. Print.

Kuchar, Gary. *The poetry of religious sorrow in early modern England*. Cambridge: Cambridge University Press. 2008. Print.

__________. *George Herbert and the Mystery of the Word: Poetry and Scripture in Seventeenth-century England*. Cham: Palgrave Macmillan. 2017. Print.

Lambert, Gregg. *Return of the Baroque in Modern Culture*. London: Continuum, 2004. Print.

Lessenich, Rolf, P. "The "Metaphysicals": English Baroque Literature in Context". Online.

Martz, Louis L. *From Renaissance to baroque: essays on literature and art*. Columbia: University of Missouri Press. 1991. Print.

Nietzsche, Friedrich. "On the Baroque style." *Human, All too Human. A Book for free spirits*. Translated by R. J. Hollingdale. Introduction by Richard Schacht. Cambridge: Cambridge University Press, 1986, 1996. Print.

Peregrini, Matteo. "Fonti dell' ingegno ridotti ad arte." (1650) Abridged in *Trattatisti e narratori del Seicento*. Ed. Ezio Raimondi. Milan: 1969. Print.

_____________. *Delle Acutezze che altrimenti spiriti, vivezze e Concetti si appellano.*(1639) Abridged in *Trattatisti e narratori del Seicento*. Ed. Ezio Raimondi. Milan: 1969.

Praz, Mario. *The Flaming Heart*. New York: Norton, 1973. Print.

Redpath, Theodore. *The Songs and Sonnets of John Donne*. Second edition. London: Methuen. 1983. Print.

Smith, J. C. "On Metaphysical Poetry," *Scrutiny*, Dec. 1933. Print.

Smith, Nigel. *The Poems of Andrew Marvell*. Harlow: Pearson Education, 2007. Print.

Tesauro, Emanuele. Il Cannocchiale Aristotelico. 1670 edition. Reprint. Hamburg, 1968.

Tuve, Rosemund. Elizabethan and Metaphysical Imagery. Chicago: University of Chicago Press, 1961. Print.

Verdicchio, Massimo. *Naming Things. Aesthetics, Philosophy and History in Benedetto Croce*. Naples: La citta del Sole, 2000. Print.

____________. "Under Western Literary Eyes: Du Fu". *Journal of Comparative Literature Studies*, Special Issue, 54.1, 2017.

Wellek, Rene. "The Concept of Baroque in Literary Scholarship". *The Journal of Aesthetics and Art Criticism*, vol. 5, no.2, Special Issue on Baroque Style in Various Arts (Dec. 1946). Print.

*****

Additional Primary and Secondary Sources (Further Reading)
Metaphysical Poets. Primary Sources:

Davis, B. E. C, and Elizabeth. *Poets of the Early Seventeenth Century.* London: Routledge & K. Paul, 1967. Print

Hill, J. P, and Caracciolo-Trejo, E. *Baroque Poetry.* London: Dent, 1975. Print

Macdonald, Hugh, ed. *The Poems of Andrew Marvell.* Cambridge, MA.: Harvard University Press, 1952. Print.

Mid-Late Tang Poetry. Primary Sources:

李賀, 李賀歌詩編：四卷. 上海：商務印書館. 1929. Print

葉蔥奇， 李賀詩集， 北京：人民文學出版社， 1959. Print

欒貴明， 張曉光， 全唐詩孟郊卷， 北京：現代出版社， 1995. Print

余恕誠, 李商隱詩, 北京：中華書局. 2014. Print

General Secondary Sources:

Alden, Raymond Macdonald. "The Lyrical Conceits of the 'Metaphysical Poets'". *Studies in Philology.* Vol. 17, no. 2 (April 1920). Print.

Bennett, Joan. *Five Metaphysical Poets.* Cambridge: Cambridge University Press, 1964. Print.

Bradbury, Malcolm and Palmer, David. *Metaphysical Poetry.* London: Edward Arnold, 1970. Print.

Davison, Dennis. "Marvell's 'The Definition of Love'," *The Review of English Studies,* Vol. 6, No. 22 (Apr., 1955), 141-146. Print.

Fletcher, Angus. *Allegory: the Theory of a Symbolic Mode.* Princeton, N.J.: Princeton University Press, 2012. Print

Gardner, Helen. *John Donne: a Collection of Critical Essays.* Englewood Cliffs, NJ: Prentice-Hall, 1962. Print.

Grierson, J. C. *Metaphysical Lyrics and Poems of the Seventeenth Century: Donne to Butler.* Selected and edited, with an Essay, by Herbert J. C. Grierson (Oxford: Clarendon Press. London; Milford) in the *Times Literary Supplement,* October 1921. Print.

Honig, Edwin. *Dark Conceit: the Making of Allegory.* Cambridge: Walker-DeBerry, 1960. Print.

Hyman, Lawrence W. "Marvell's "Coy Mistress" and Desperate Lover". *Modern Language Notes.* Vol. 75, No. 1 (Jan., 1960), 8-10. Print.

Legouis, Pierre. "Marvell and Massinger: A Source of 'The Definition of Love'". *The Review of English Studies.* Vol. 23, No. 89 (Jan., 1947), 63-65. Print.

Moses, William Robert. *The Metaphysical Conceit in the Poems of John Donne.* Norwood, Pa.: Norwood Editions, 1977. Print.

Nelson, Lowry. *Baroque Lyric Poetry.* New Haven: Yale University Press, 1961. Print.

Ruthven, K. K. *The Conceit.* London: Methuen, 1969. Print.

Smith, A. J. *Metaphysical Wit.* Cambridge: Cambridge University Press, 1991. Print.

Warnke, Frank J. *European Metaphysical Poetry.* New Haven: Published for the Elizabethan Club. New Haven: Yale University Press, 1961. Print.

Zamora, Lois Parkinson, and Monika Kaup. *Baroque New Worlds: Representation, Transculturation, Counterconquest.* Durham, NC: Duke University Press, 2010. Print

Zunder, William. *The Poetry of John Donne: Literature and Culture in the Elizabethan and Jacobean Period.* Brighton, Sussex: Harvester Press, 1982. Print

Mid-Late Tang Poetry, Secondary Sources:

楊文雄, 李賀詩研究, 台北：文史哲出版社. 1980. Print.

董乃斌, 李商隱傳, 西安：陝西人民出版社. 1985. Print.

楊周翰, 鏡子與七巧板, 北京：中國社會科學出版社. 1990. Print.

葉蔥奇, 李商隱詩集疏注, 北京：人民文學出版社. 1998. Print.

孟二冬, 韓孟詩傳, 長春：吉林人民出版社. 2003. Print.

陳允吉, 李賀詩選評, 上海：上海古籍出版社. 2004. Print.

吳企明, 李賀資料彙編, 北京：中華書局. 2004. Print.

莊蕙綺, 中唐詩歌的美學意涵, 台北：新文豐. 2006. Print.

張宗福, 李賀研究, 成都：巴蜀書社. 2009. Print.

朱自清. 李賀年譜, 清華學報, 北京, 1935, 4, 887 - 915.

Index

I

J

K

L

M

N

O

P

Q

R

S

T

W

X

Y

Z

www.ingramcontent.com/pod-product-compliance
Lightning Source LLC
LaVergne TN
LVHW020641100826
845148LV00012B/2290
9781622739585